T0355895

THE
TEAM
THAT COULD
HAVE BEEN

Stephen Brandt

THE
TEAM
THAT COULD
HAVE BEEN

The Rise and Fall of
Crystal Palace's
Team of the 80s

First published by Pitch Publishing, 2024

Pitch Publishing
9 Donnington Park,
85 Birdham Road,
Chichester,
West Sussex,
PO20 7AJ
www.pitchpublishing.co.uk
info@pitchpublishing.co.uk

A CIP catalogue record is available for this book
from the British Library.

ISBN 978 1 80150 663 2

Typesetting and origination by Pitch Publishing

Printed and bound in India by Thomson Press

Contents

To Dad. Thank you.

Preface

THE FOOTBALL nostalgia genre has exploded over the past decade. Many clubs have hundreds of books out on their glory eras – just stop by any newsagent or bookstore. The number of Barcelona, Bayern Munich, Celtic, Liverpool, Everton, Arsenal and Manchester United books out there is massive. Writing about the good times is fun, and very fruitful for many people. A retelling of a great night for a great club is what writers want.

Then there's writing about the times, the eras in which a club should have done well but couldn't get out of their own way. That takes longer and is much harder. It's more fulfilling and relaxing in the end. Bringing out why something happened, while finding the good stories grows a writer's craft more than anything. Some clubs just have a hard time during their existence, and this isn't a book about Leeds.

That's where *The Team of the 80s* book came from. Crystal Palace have books out about the club, and all of them are good. BT Sport produced a documentary on them in 2019, and it was very well done. However, there was, strangely, nothing out about the team, despite many of the players being quite famous or personable. Many of the Palace fan blogs and message boards have long threads of their memories of the club.

For me as an American it was something I felt more people needed to hear about. That era, the background information and filler material was abundant. Sadly, due to how culture has decided to make social media and common discourse, approaching people was very hard during 2020–22 when I wrote the book. However, Crystal Palace, TheEaglesBeak blog, and Five Year Plan were all more than helpful for background information. As an aside, Palace supporters have always been the most welcoming and helpful for an American getting into the sport. I haven't met a bad apple in any of them. From the early days of writing, TheEaglesBeak was there for my scribblings and developing love for the sport. While this book is dedicated to other people, it's written for the good people who have supported the club through thick and thin.

Stephen Brandt

Chapter 1

The Crystal Palace

TO START a history book on Crystal Palace Football Club, we need to get to the origins of the name of the club. It starts back in Victorian London and the Crystal Palace. The structure has been on the badge on the club's shirts for years, even though, as we'll find out, the building hasn't been around for a while. The structure was built during the Victorian era, a period of optimism and unlimited ways to be good. The Georgian era that preceded it included the Industrial Revolution and had assured Britain's position at the top of the manufacturing world. Prince Albert, the husband of Queen Victoria, became the President of the Society of Arts in 1847 and played an important part in mounting a series of manufacturing exhibitions to show off all the good in British life. It was the vision of Henry Cole, the Assistant Keeper of the Records Office, who was responsible for promoting such exhibitions.

Cole was a man of many talents: painter, author, architect, historian. In his mind, after gathering all the information, he considered the possibility of Britain staging an international exhibition of a size not realised before. This would become the world's largest greenhouse, the Crystal Palace. Like any new proposition, there was much opposition, but once they got the naysayers to figure it out, they had to find a site to stage it. The site picked for the hall was Hyde Park, and the building had to be designed so that it was capable of housing manufacturing goods from around the world. Money had to be raised and, due to legislation, all this was done over an 18-month timeframe.

In Victorian Britain all this was possible, with a Royal Commission overseeing the process. They raised the money through public subscription, and everyone from the richest to the poorest had to contribute to the cause, raising £79,000, underwritten by £250,000 from manufacturers. The design was commissioned by architects Thomas Leverton Donaldson and Charles Barry. The engineers were the best too: Robert Stephenson and Isambard Kingdom Brunel. But the project failed and it looked as though Britain would have egg on its face.

Then Joseph Paxton came along to save the day. He was an architect who specialised in building with glass and iron. He was a self-made, self-taught man, creating the most spectacular buildings the world would ever see. Paxton started working as a gardener at Chiswick, until he was noticed by the Duke of Devonshire. Paxton became a friend, and a manager of the duke's estates.

The interest in glass and iron buildings came out of a happy occurrence, trying to find a structure for plant cutting propagation at Chatsworth.

Paxton didn't plan to become involved with the exhibition, but a discussion in London with John Ellis MP made him think otherwise. He was, however, given two weeks to put together a plan with detailed drawings. As a self-made man, he was able to do things quickly with great competence, and the first sketch was drawn in minutes. Also, the fact that Paxton could turn to British manufacturers of iron and glass to bring this to life, while getting the quality and quantity of goods, was impressive.

Paxton's design needed 205 miles of sash bars, 2,150 iron girders, 3,300 columns, 600,000 cubic feet of timbers to create the sparkle, and 900,000 square feet of glass. The supply list was amazing, to be transported from Birmingham to London. The building would cover 19 acres of land and enclose 33 million cubic feet. The cathedral-like structure consisted of nave and transepts, along with galleries. Each piece of the build had to be hauled into place via men and horses, levers and pulleys. Teams of men worked in unison, 2,000 of them on site at full steam. The panels were moved into position using trolleys that ran along the guttering pipes, all 34 miles of them. The glaziers' skilled work was followed by teams of painters. Then there were joiners, fixing the stalls for the 14,000 exhibitors – 11 miles of stalls. This was all accomplished in nine months, while nowadays things take years to finish. And we have better tools these days.

With just weeks to go, the great Crystal Palace was home to a flock of London sparrows, enjoying the conditions inside among the elm trees. This would be a disaster, because no one would want bird droppings on the artefacts. Queen Victoria, with the Duke of Wellington inspected the problem. He said they should install sparrow hawks, solving the issue.

In 1851 the exhibition saw over six million people file through the great building. Although it didn't meet the aims of increased trade, it did bring together what would become a legacy of art and design to that part of London. Paxton wanted the Palace to stay put, as he didn't want his masterpiece to come down, so he raised over £500,000 to buy, move and expand the structure to a site at Sydenham Hill, which had commanding views of London. It was known as the Winter Palace, and it would house great art, exotic plants, temples and fountains. It would also be the showcase for great civilisations, art and architecture. It eventually became five storeys, although the capacity was half as much as it was supposed to be originally. The water towers, heating, landscaping and so much more meant the total cost reached several million pounds.

Brunel, the great engineer, became part of the exhibition. He built the water towers, each able to hold 30,000 tons of water. That load meant the foundations had to be dug very deep and Portland cement had to be laid. Tanks that supplied water for the fountains and integrated the pumping system were needed, a feat of incredible engineering. The scale of this exhibition defied belief but not efficiency, nor success. They averaged a visitor count of two million each year for 30 years but it was still a huge expenditure to maintain.

The end came for the Crystal Palace on 1 December 1936 at six o'clock in the evening. A small fire started in a toilet and within half an hour spread throughout the building, eating away through the wood of the floors and walls. As the force of the fire blasted the glass from the structure, thousands of people gathered outside to see the collapsing of the building. Remember, spectacles create big business.

Many people saw the site as a way to make money, or to claim it for themselves. During the Second World War it was used as anti-aircraft gun emplacement and military storage. After the war, London's South Bank, rather than Sydenham, was chosen as the site for the 1951 Festival of Britain. The Crystal Palace Park was proposed to be the new home for the Festival Dome of Discovery and Skylon but was rejected. The park did attract new investment, though, as the National Recreation Centre and a concert bowl were added in the 1960s. But the site of Paxton's gem remained empty, save for a television station in the 1950s. The garden terraces and one of the Brunel water towers still stood.

In the 2010s a well-supported plan to reconstruct the Crystal Palace was abandoned. Chinese developer

Zhongrong Group failed to meet the required criteria and a 16-month deadline set by London Borough of Bromley. They had planned to restore the spirit, scale and magnificence of the original. They had top architects, Zaha Hadid and David Chipperfield, to submit proposals, but it was going to be a slow process. To date the property still hasn't been rebuilt.

For the last four years of the 1930s, uncertainty dominated. The Blitz also later made the property a landfill for the city. There were numerous imitations, including one in New York City, and the proposal by Charles Burton for a 1,000-foot Crystal Tower in London. However, by the time the palace burned down, the world of architecture had moved on.

Chapter 2

Setting the Scene

THE 1970s wasn't a good era for portions of society. When the 'Team of the 80s' were finding their feet, they were doing so against the backdrop of social strife, racism in the game and an uncertain daily existence. Croydon, where the club is based, is a tough area to live. While London may be the capital of England, the borough of Croydon isn't on any tour guide's map. That's not knocking it as a bad place. It's one of the boroughs of London, if we couch it in how Americans refer to parts of big cities. Couched in British terms, it's a parish of London, and it's to the south of the city by about nine miles. The neighbourhood of Croydon is steeped in prehistoric and nearly historic remains, with hut floors among them. The remains could have come over from the early Roman Empire. There are also copper coins from different dates BC, which could show a line of traffic throughout England.

As with anything old or historic, there were skirmishes in Croydon; for example, in 1264 when Londoners were driven off the field at Lewes. William, the only son of John de Warenne, Earl of Surrey, was killed in 1266 at Croydon. The original village, like most villages at the time, stood around a church, and was on the Thanet and Woolwich beds of chalk. Famous people of the time, such as the archbishops of Canterbury, lived there. It was the centre for the management of archiepiscopal estates in Surrey, Middlesex and Hertfordshire. We don't know how long ago the archbishops kept a house in Croydon, but we can go back at least as far as 1273. We do know there was a house there at least a century earlier, and the archbishops could have been there before that time. Most of them used the residence as a summer retreat or a place to entertain guests.

James I of Scotland dated a deed at Croydon in 1412 when he was staying at the palace during the custody of Archbishop Arundel. In 1957 Queen Elizabeth II came to Croydon from Greenwich, and stayed a week with her attendants. The palace had convenient access to London, but it became less fashionable to stay there over the years and was sold to Abraham Pitches of Streatham on 10 October 1780. In 1818 the palace was used as a factory for printing linen, the garden being turned into a bleaching ground. It's still standing to this day.

The events of the Battle of Britain ravaged many areas of the country, and the Blitz took down many buildings in London. During the Second World War, Croydon had an airport, the main one for London at the time. However, during this time much of Croydon was destroyed by German V-1 flying bombs and V-2 rockets. Once the war was over, Heathrow Airport took Croydon's place. The space hasn't been wasted, though, as in 2000 the Croydon Airport Visitor Centre was opened to chart the history of the airport from the First World War to its closure in 1959.

The time period we're mostly going to be talking about is the 1970s, an era of deep trouble in all parts of the UK. Population shifts led, as they often do, to changing demographics. The 1970s saw more Britons from traditional London move further away from the city centre, with many of these people being Black or recent immigrants. Campaigners and Black citizens have been met with violence, threats and horrible behaviour, but this has all made Croydon the great area it has become.

One of the problems with society was the publishing of Darwin's theory on natural selection, which was, in simple terms, the inheritance of dominant traits over subordinate traits for survival. It's not applied in Darwin's sense to humans but, for Victorian and modern-day society, others have used it that way. Social Darwinism is the belief that certain people become powerful ... read that as Caucasians, because they're better. While this has been debunked, it's still used as a basis for how Black people were and are treated. The father of eugenics, Francis Galton, said that Darwin's theory helped in his thinking down his road of expertise. What Galton proposed was the removal of nature to determine what traits would be descended down the generations of humans; in other words, removing Black people. Inferior races need not exist anymore … a very scary proposition.

Thomas Huxley was another advocate of Darwin's theory. His focus was mainly within the field of physical anthropology, as an ability to seek an answer to man's place in nature. Huxley was studying the brain and bone structure of various different races of humans, to compare them to apes. He concluded that men evolved from apes, which was not racist in nature, but he did say there were differences between the brains and bones of White Europeans and Africans. Huxley attached the idea of racial inequality to those discoveries, fuelling the idea of White superiority. Huxley didn't hide the fact that he thought the White race was superior. He made such racist claims into common knowledge because he was leader of the Anthropological Institute of Great Britain and Ireland. By having someone in high positions of power it became institutionalised and professionalised.

More Black Britons and immigrants moved in the community, but Croydon had historically been a conservative, White, middle-class suburb. It had deep connections to the British fascist group, A.K. Chesterton's League of Empire Loyals, which was based in Chesterton's home in south Croydon. There was also John Tyndall's National Labour Party, based in Thornton Heath. These two men played critical roles in the formation of the National Front, with their office based at 50 Pawsons Road in Thornton Heath in 1972.

Despite all this, Thornton Heath did witness significant efforts to support those moving into South London. Parchmore Methodist Church was one such group that helped lead the way, although they were frustrated as the 1970s proceeded as they received limited help from the left wing. Along the lines of the Methodist Church, the Croydon Black Marxist Collective established *Frontlines*, a newspaper based out of the former Black Panther headquarters in South Norwood.

As the decades changed, the despair and anger among the British spilled over, and 1981 was a very disturbing year of riots around the country.[1] This was also the decade during which hooliganism was rife within football. While the UK was an open society, it was open to only what it wanted. In 1981 the totality of misery and desperation produced a year of people seemingly having nothing better to do than riot for their rights. During the first part of July 1981 every major city and town was hit by youth riots, where bored people readied themselves for nights of burning and looting. Kids as young as eight were arrested in Manchester for setting fire to a bike shop. A paraplegic elderly person was propelled into a supermarket so he could be involved in the looting in Bristol.

Policing in London was considered poor, highlighted by the 9 August 1970 group of Black Power activists who

---

1 'This Week in UK History, 1981: Uprisings and Riots all over the Country', Past Tense Publications. Blog at WordPress.com. 3 July 2021.

led 150 people on a march against police harassment in the Black community in Notting Hill, London. They wanted an end to the persecution of the Mangrove Restaurant, which the police had raided 12 times between January 1969 and July 1970. No illegal activity was found there but the local constabulary remained convinced there was trouble at the restaurant. At the protest march, violence broke out. The following year, the Mangrove Nine were put on trial but were acquitted of the most serious charges after a 55-day trial.

Society made life hard for young Black youths in the 70s. The police viewed inner-city locations and gathering points as troublesome and criminal. Street robberies were a new concern for people, so anytime they saw youths together, it was pearl-clutching time. The police aggressively stopped and searched Black youths for no reason, just on the view that something bad might happen.

The killing of Blair Peach by a police officer flamed the hatred of the force by all races too. On 23 April 1979, Blair was protesting against the National Front at Southall. The protest had been set up weeks before, when the Tory-run London Borough of Ealing allowed the National Front to hold its election meeting in the town hall. The Indian Workers Association called a meeting with their president Vishnu Sharma, at which they raised a petition demanding that the council should ban the National Front. They planned to hold a protest to hand over the petition to the local authority. If the National

Front meeting wasn't cancelled, then they would ask all the local workers to go on strike at midday on Monday, 23 April. During the rally the youth had a peaceful sit-down protest against the National Front.

Finally, on 22 April, 5,000 people assembled to begin the protest march under a massive police presence, who were there apparently to protect the marchers, but their true nature was soon revealed. The police began to harass the marchers outside Southall Police Station, arresting a young Black man for being a bit excited. Eventually, when cooler heads prevailed, the young man was released from police custody. By the time the march got past Ealing hospital the police had become more and more aggressive, and scuffles broke out. They arrested 15 people, with much of the commotion apparently started by the police.

In readiness for 23 April, the police arrived in numbers – 3,000 of them. They were even more aggressive during the second day of marching. Then at 1pm all the local shops and local businesses were shut and the workers went on strike too. The police tried to smuggle the National Front into the town hall, which caused the protesters to surge forward, leading to the police becoming more aggressive.

The police then refused to cooperate with the protest, because they were in full battle mode. The siege of Southall was on, with more and more people arriving to demand what was right in the world. As more people showed up, the police set up roadblocks away from the town hall. The protesters were mostly local, young and old, of all genders and races. All came to show their solidarity. Residents weren't even allowed to go to their own homes. As the restlessness was ramped up, and they were breaking through the police lines, the police became more angry. A Special Patrol Group (SPG) was added to the crowd, with a van of that unit speeding towards the group. They threw anyone in sight into the vans.

The police with dogs then began to chase people. So with all of this going on, protesters showed up with bricks and anything else to fight back against the police. This went on for many hours. As night fell, the police set off some flares and were also hitting people over the head with truncheons. They attacked everyone, including the manager of a reggae band, Clarence Baker. Around 7.30pm, many of the National Front were giving Nazi salutes and shouting racist tropes to stand their ground. This enraged many protesters and led to more violent police attacks.

Blair Peach and his friends were trapped by an SPG group at Orchard Avenue. Six people saw an SPG police officer club Peach over the head, knocking him to the ground. The Atwai family called for an ambulance, but Peach died in Ealing hospital due to the blow to his head. Nearly 700 people were arrested, but only 342 were charged. Peach was part of the Anti-Nazi League and well known in the community as a lad who would be out helping. The media was blaming outsiders, not the police. To this day no one has been charged with the murder, even though many have tried to get the records opened up to achieve some justice for Blair.

Policing in the inner cities was particularly troubling at the time. This was due to the violent paramilitary policing of the inner-city communities. Behind all this was abject poverty, desperation and work in big cities drying up. Manufacturing jobs became increasingly scarce and many people ended up on the dole. We had a generation who could see that life was all about being poor and treated poorly. It seemed the only way they could stick it to the man was to smash things, so there were many areas, not limited to the capital, where riots kicked off.

On 2 April 1980 at 3.30pm Bristol saw a riot that kicked off at St Pauls and Southmead but, when digging deeper, you find more. The underground scene has always been key in driving British music to the forefront. This was from 70s post-punk, to reggae, to hip-hop and the development of trip-hop. In 1979 young kids would leave school, and like a lot of the country were unemployed. They had nothing to do but hang around, which caused unrest, but also created the club reggae and dub voices that fired up a nation of the missed youth. The St Pauls riots had a strong impact on the evolution of the underground scene. Many bands, such as Untouchables, Private Number and Sonic Invaders, helped influence the Black Roots. They weren't the first reggae band, but they were the first significant recording artist. Their militant pacifism struck a chord with people who were in a time of strife and social conflict.

Bristol during the mid-70s was a fairly segregated city, but people didn't like to talk about it. Then the riot erupted and reggae saw a moment to inspire a nation. The climate of resistance to oppression, inequality, unemployment, racial injustice and police brutality was in each song. This fiery streak remains and maintains Bristol as a multicultural melting pot burning today.

Before we get into what happened later, in the early 80s, let's circle back to Bristol in 1980 when the police with 20 officers raided the Black and White Cafe. They did so suspecting drug dealing in the St Pauls building. The violent riots ended with 21 people arrested and 33 people injured.[2] There are many theories out there about how the rioting started when the police showed up, but as the mood went from moderate to angry, the crowd became bigger, increasing into the thousands.

Bricks and bottles were used as weapons by the rioters, bringing in extra police officers, who showed up without riot gear. Their substitute was dustbin lids to shield themselves from the objects being thrown at them. Almost two hours later, at 5.15pm, the riot was still going and had spread to nearby Ashley Road and City, where the police were cornered due to the number of rioters. The rioting became worse as the day went on. More and more police arrived, but this time they brought their riot shields. The bank was hit, a post office, a row of shops and a warehouse on Brighton Street, all on the

2   Laura Churchill. 'St. Paul's Riots 37 Years On', Bristol Live/*Bristol Post*. 3 April 2017.

hit list of the rioters. Two hours later, at 7.30pm, the riot was still not under control. Firefighters were also trying to put out the fires from all the police cars going up in flames.

By 11pm the police, who had been withdrawn a couple of hours previously, came back with a plan – and 200 officers, mostly borrowed from neighbouring constabularies. They set up roadblocks around the perimeter of St Pauls, the M32 roundabout and Stokes Croft, which stopped people coming and going into the danger zone. Just before midnight, St Pauls calmed down and the crowds left the area. The outcome was 33 people injured, plus 12 police cars and several fire engines damaged, mostly by fire. Property damage was in the thousands of pounds, and there was much looting from shops. The police arrested 21 people, but there were no convictions.

In South London, the Black community also exploded into the early 80s insurgency. On 18 January 1981, the New Cross house fire brought more anger to the country. Thirteen Black youths, all between 15 and 20 years old, were killed in a fire during a birthday party for Yvonne Ruddock (16) and Angela Jackson (18) at 439 New Cross Road in Deptford, South London. The police originally thought it was a fire caused by a firebomb. Most in the community thought it was a racist attack, since firebombing had been endemic against the Black and Asian communities during the 70s. The local Black community felt the attack was ignored by the elite and the police, who started turning on the community. Anger grew in the area among the Black community, resulting in the Black People's Day of Action on Monday, 2 March.

Between 3,000 and 6,000 people, the majority of them Black, took part in the event in London. It was a demonstration organised by the New Cross Massacre Action Committee as a protest against the police's handling of the Deptford fire investigation. The demonstration was a watershed moment in rioting. Just like today, police, government and establishment media were quick to label the events of 1981 all about race; however, in many of the uprisings, Whites fought alongside Blacks and Asians. A sense of community was key in beating back the hate. The press named it the Deptford fire, but Black Power and the left-wing political activists called it the New Cross Massacre. That was because they believed that the tragedy was caused by a racist arson attack.

We're uncertain of the cause of the fire but two things are obvious: the victims weren't to blame, and the aftermath of the tragedy showed the continuing and corrosive effects of racism in the UK. The media and government's hostile response helped stoke the fires of violence and racism towards Black Britons in the decades after the Second World War. While the war was many decades before the Team of the 80s was even thought of, the hatred for others was ingrained in the souls of multigenerational Britons.

The start of the 1981 events was the now-famous riot in Brixton, South London. Officially, the area was patrolled by an army of police to crack down on street crime. The Met Police named the programme 'Operation Swamp 81'.[3] In reality, the programme was deemed as a cover for the police to harass, arrest and beat up Black youths. It backfired big time, because during 10 and 13 April the riot kicked off. On Friday, 10 April the police were attacked by a group of 40–50 youths. Over the following three days, violence flared and rioters set fire to 26 buildings, one fire engine and 19 cars. Between 145 and 165 police were injured during the riots. There were nearly 200 arrests and 226 casualties. Damage was rumoured to be valued at between £2 million and £10 million. By the following Monday the riot had calmed down and no further arrests were made.

Sure enough, further rioting kicked off not a week later, over Easter weekend, 17–20 April. This, however, wasn't just at one location, it was in numerous seaside resorts. Gangs of mods, skinheads, punks and rockers or, as most people would say, anti-establishment types, hit many resorts. It was a situation in which very few could tell who was doing what, but it was all over the place.

In Southend a large number of skinheads gathered for the weekend. Shop windows were smashed and 170 people were arrested.[4] In Margate there were 39 arrests,

---

3   Perry Blankston. 'The Great Insurrection: Remembering the Brixton Uprising', *The Tribune*. 11 April 2023.

4   'This Week in UK History, 1981: Uprisings and Riots all over the Country', Past Tense Publications. Blog at WordPress.com. 3 July 2021.

with only one police officer and one skinhead injured. In Hastings 20 people were arrested after clashes between rival gangs. In the popular coastal resort of Brighton all police leave was cancelled as 1,000 mods arrived. There were 92 arrests over the weekend. Some other resorts were hit too: Great Yarmouth saw 40 arrests, and Scarborough 78.

Then the London fairs were brought into the conversation, mostly involving Black youths. At Finsbury Park, reportedly, 500 Black teenagers attacked shops and fought police outside the fairground.[5] Eight police and 20 civilians were injured, 40 people arrested and £1,000 of electrical goods looted from one of the shops. Meanwhile, at Ealing Common, 300 Black youths smashed shop windows and damaged police cars.

In Coventry on 23 May, during a march of 8,000 Asians protesting against the racist attacks in the city, violence broke out, as 200 skinheads shouted fascist slogans and heckled the marchers. The skinheads fought with 1,500 police officers patrolling the march. Over 70 people were arrested, and one police officer was stabbed.

On 1 June in Thornton Heath, South London, local Black youths attacked the Wilton Arms pub looking for the National Front, to avenge racist attacks. One youth was killed in the street. Later that day, eight police officers were injured in a clash with Black youths at a shopping centre in Lewisham, south-east London. The

---

5   This Week in UK History, 1981: Uprisings and Riots all over the Country', Past Tense Publications. Blog at WordPress.com. 3 July 2021.

trouble in Lewisham spilled over into the next day, as the police arrested a girl in the shopping centre and were attacked by Black youths. Ten people were arrested and 100 youths gathered in front of the police station, shouting abuse. It was close to a riot. At this point many would have been weary of the constant riots and demonstrations, so you can see the backdrop of what the Crystal Palace players were dealing with. Seeing their society being torn down on a day-to-day basis would wear on anyone, and make the victories on the pitch much sweeter.

It didn't stop there, though, as on 20 June the fairground in Peckham Rye Common was hit by 1,000 youths. Thirty shop windows were smashed and 28 people were arrested. Then on 3 July, Southall erupted when skinheads were bussed into an area with a heavy Asian and Black population. A concert by the band Oil at Hambrough Tavern was taking place at the same time. The skinheads marched on High Street, smashing windows and harassing people. The West London's Asian Youth Movement laid siege to the pub. When the police arrived, there were over 100 casualties, 61 of them police officers.

The Toxteth Riots also kicked off in July; some of the most well-known riots. Late on Saturday, 4 July, violence broke out in Liverpool 8, Toxteth. Police were checking on a report of a stolen car, which then turned into a full-blown attack, as 200 Black and White youths, some wearing balaclavas, built barricades, threw petrol bombs and used vehicles as battering rams to break the police lines. A school and several shops were burned to the ground.

It didn't get any better, as on the following day the rioting raged out of control. The police called in reinforcements from over the north-west. Seeing widespread society fight back against the fascism of the state gave rise to the chanting on the football terraces to fight back against the establishment. The local community poured out into the streets to loot everything they could. They had shopping trolleys, filling them with whatever they could find. They used vans to pick up anything that could fill the back of the vehicles. CS gas was used well into the early hours of Monday to disperse the rioters.

The violence continued the next day, but with far less intensity than the previous two nights. There was a mix of many races rioting, but reportedly only the Caucasians were looting. The damage was 255 police officers injured, with 70 people appearing in court on the Monday, then a further 77 on Tuesday. Most were Caucasian, some as young as 13.

There were also, from time, to time copycat riots, such as in Wood Green, North London, involving 200 youths, mainly Black and Greek Cypriot. On 7 July, between 400 and 500 youths looted shops in Wood Green and attacked the police. The newspapers stated that the same number of youths, this time Black, gathered near Turnpike Lane underground station and marched along High Road. The SPG was called in, carrying riot shields, trying to drive the youths back. Eventually, the 10pm news reported the incident and the crowd soon increased. In total, 35 shops on the Wood Green High Road were looted or had their windows broken. Various reports had 26 police officers injured and 50 civilians arrested.

Riots and racial tensions kicked off in various hotspots in the country for the rest of the month. On 10 July, 200 Black and Asian youths ran through the town centre, smashing 15 shop windows and overturning cars. There was also some looting. The youths outnumbered the police, and 27 arrests were made. The events seem to have been provoked by rumours of a skinhead invasion because of a concert at Tramshed. There was some truth to the rumours, because there was a similar occurrence the week before in Southall. This seemed to be a normal, daily event in Woolwich. The British Movement had been very active in the area before these events. Nicci Crane, an English neo-Nazi activist, was later jailed for four years for his part in an attack on Black youths at Woolwich Arsenal station.

The UK government dealt with the prolonged riots by imposing strict rules. The Thatcher administration was harsh on many things, and this was to be another feather in her cap. Jails were overcrowded already, to a point where there were proposals to create overflow arrangements in old army camps. To tackle the problem, one could look at the sentencing issues. Some were there on short sentences with little to no defence, or long sentences for criminal damage, or maybe Molotov cocktail offences. Some conformity among the magistrates could have calmed the voice of anger a bit. We're also only a decade away from Hillsborough, Heysel and Thatcher effectively taking steps to criminalise football supporters.

The *Huffington Post*, decades later, reported a speech by Prime Minister Thatcher:

> 'We really must eradicate the blot on our reputation,' said Margaret Thatcher, the former British prime minister who died last week. The Iron Lady was referring to English soccer hooligans as if they were enemies of the state. Stitch the sociology pattern. The Iron Lady ripped up Britain's post-war social contract while serving as British prime minister from 1979–1990. The country was sharply divided ideologically and regionally. Left-wing trade unions were crushed, industry privatised, capital unleashed, the dole was as popular as pop music. Add the drums of class war – Margaret Thatcher was the ultimate class warrior, divide and rule. Her legacy was violence, and soccer was on the frontline.[6]

This era was the start of the problems for the Thatcher government, and she was trying to mould the UK into

---

6   A.M. Black. 'Soccer under Thatcher: Violence, Tragedy and Transformation', *Huffington Post*. 16 April 2013.

a nation that didn't have anything that could bring the country bad press. But seeing the elite or establishment take such a strict stance on everyday life fuelled the riots, the chanting and troubles between football supporters.

The National Front was led by John Tyndall, who openly worshipped Hitler. The organisation was fascist to its core, but also had a strong section of Tories and others who could not understand that the UK had lost so much world power during the post-war era. However, in the 1979 general election, the Tories won, and the National Front, while standing a record number of candidates, failed to win any seats and collapsed altogether. It's no surprise that after the original National Front fell apart, Tyndall formed another party, the British National Party, in 1982. It struggled to find a foothold in the political spectrum well into the 90s.

The ideas being implemented were still not bringing the obvious issues to the forefront. There were failed proposals to bring back the Riot Act, which stated that anyone present at the scene of a riot would be jailed automatically without a jury trial. Also in the running were proposals to arm the police, which also came to nothing. The government had a problem, as all this rioting came a couple of years after the 'Winter of Discontent'. But the riots of 81 helped the Tory government with the narrative of 'enemies within'. Basically, anyone they didn't like was an enemy. The government concluded that new public order arrangements should be put in place: specialist police uniforms, helmets, riot shields and equipment. There was also specific training to help officers control public order situations. All of this new, albeit potentially paramilitary policing, became the norm.

Bills were also introduced to reinforce these actions, such as the 1984 Police and Criminal Evidence Act (PACE), which brought in new codes of behaviour, and a new Police Complaints Authority was set up. Legislation beefed up the police's stop and search powers with more discretion, and clauses gave the police greater control over public order problems such as riots, picket lines and demonstrations.

Added to this, the government wanted to know exactly why the rioting was happening. They realised that tens of thousands of people do not riot without reason, so it at least needed looking into. The Right Honourable Lord Scarman was commissioned to do this. He concluded that the ethnic communities in the UK's inner cities felt they had little impact on life. Their relationships with the institutions, especially with the police, had broken down, and changes were needed. So it wasn't the police's fault after all.

To bring about improvements for the urban youth, programmes were brought in after 1981. Mostly these were private partnerships and regeneration projects, aiming to get young unemployed people into jobs, albeit low-paying ones, or Youth Training Schemes. It was simply a way for employers to exploit people who had left school without qualifications, without having to provide real training or education.

The minority populations in large cities worldwide were concentrated in ghettos, which were more or less the poorer areas with the worst accommodation, and there were bleak job prospects. All this could be defined as a deep-rooted form of injustice. So many people had little stake in society and lived with miserable economic prospects, so the potential for unrest was evident. The Thatcher government can be criticised for many things, one of which was its policies in this area. For the most part, at the localised level, policing tactics in the poorest inner-city areas saw Black youths targeted the most and in the most brutal ways. This created anti-police resentment and mutual hostility between police and the local population.

One of the great books on racism in the UK is Paul Gilroy's *There Ain't No Black in the Union Jack: The Cultural Politics of Race and Nation*. It's a damaging thesis on contemporary attitudes to race, and one that the politicians and elite failed to take race seriously. The title comes from a football terrace chant heard during England international matches. The double standards of imperialism made Britain the 'motherland', while trying to keep those conquered countries at arm's length from coming to the 'motherland'. This is why for a long time several good Black footballers failed to break through into the national team.

British nationalism is centred on Englishness as being White, but Gilroy's book puts the narrative that multiculturalism is what makes Britain as good as it is. This is what brought football out of the boring, grind-it-out type of play into what we see today. Despite all this, there's no effective way to confront the past, and those who cling on to it are stubborn enough to not like the changes that have come about. The media and the legal system still maintain racism. Repeating 'go back home' is also a false narrative, because where is home, if they were born in the country that does not want them? When society is at its height, and doing well, all nationalities, races and sexes are working together in harmony.

Rock Against Racism (RAR), a movement that was active from 1976 to 1980, was a collective of activists and musicians who put together more than 500 concerts across the UK. There were marches of almost 100,000 supporters, and bands such as The Clash and Steel Pulse played. The tour was named the Militant Entertainment, and one part of it brought thousands of people to the beach in Norfolk.

The first gig was in November 1976 at the Princess Alice pub on Commercial Street in Aldgate, London. Performers included reggae band Matumbi from South London, and jazz singer Carol Grimes. This galvanised local RAR groups to set up their own concerts around the country, such as the Carnival Against the Nazis in Victoria Park, East London. On 30 April 1978 roughly 100,000 people marched seven miles from Trafalgar Square and rocked out against the National Front, and people like Enoch Powell. The Clash shared the stage with Patrick Fitzgerald, X-Ray Spex, the Tom Robinson Band and Steel Pulse. There was a clear energy beyond the music that day. Protest is a fluid word and concept, when it takes on righteousness; it flows within.

Not too long after the concert, Altab Ali was murdered in Whitechapel park. Ten days later, 7,000 people marched behind Ali's coffin to Downing Street, chanting 'unite and fight'. With the tensions boiling, they then burst into the open, bracing for more turbulence. These were the moments in history where passions come together to create something mighty, even if it is brief.

Eventually, The Clash, known for their nonconforming political stance, stoked the fires of the Anti-Nazi League. The event was conceived in 1976 by Red Saunders, Roger Huddle, Jo Wreford, Pete Bruno and others, but was just an idea for a while, not a reality. What got it off the ground was the hypocrisies of Eric Clapton, a skilled but angry musician, who had been influenced by Black musicians but was now leaning towards the racist political figure of Enoch Powell. At a gig in Birmingham he suggested that Powell's Rivers of Blood speech was right, and he was repeating the National Front's slogan.

RAR was only able to get off the ground through a groundswell of support. The theatre groups started expressing their opposition to Clapton's remarks by firing off a letter explaining the hypocrisy of his stance. This letter was the start of RAR, and hundreds of replies wanted an end to the hypocrisy. RAR, to keep the momentum going after the first gig, reached into football fandom and released a fanzine called *Temporary Housing*.

The growth of RAR also coincided with the rise of punk and its groups popping up all over the country. These RAR groups were showing up in Leeds, Birmingham, Manchester, Hull, Newcastle, Edinburgh, Glasgow, Belfast, Sheffield, Cardiff, Swansea, Bristol and London. Eventually there were 200 events throughout the UK and several in other countries around the world. By 1978 they needed to go bigger, so they looked into the idea of a carnival organised alongside the Anti-Nazi League, to thumb their nose at the rise of racist attacks in the UK. Two carnivals were held in poor but culturally rich areas. The first was 30 April at Victoria Park. The Clash performed 'White Riot' and 'London's Burning'. The crowd included 42 coaches from Glasgow, 15 from Sheffield and an entire trainload from Manchester. Through this outpouring of success and energy at the concert, years later Live Aid came about.

But Clapton wasn't the only one who was expounding on those racist terms, or using the Nazi symbols for shock. Soon this would include Sid Vicious, Siouxsie Sioux and even David Bowie. All this vileness was hard to watch, especially when David Bowie gave an interview to Cameron Crowe in a 1976 for *Playboy* saying he was a very strong believer of fascism. Bowie even went on to call Hitler a rock star, but perhaps this was just one of

Bowie's different personas that he took on over his career. He did, however, say that he wasn't a fascist. You decide.

After a carnival in Leeds that was headlined by The Specials, RAR was disbanded. However, that wasn't the last we would hear of the organisation. In 2002 it was revived and renamed Love Music Hate Racism. This was the organisation behind the 30th-anniversary concert in Victoria Park, with the supergroup The Good, the Bad, and the Queen, which included former Clash guitarist Paul Simonon.

The rioting was finally brought under control, gradually, over the summer weeks, but the damage left in its wake was felt for a very long time. On the positive side, it helped rejuvenate previously depressed and downtrodden inner-city areas through programmes over a longer term. Well-known examples include the dockland areas of London, Liverpool and Manchester/Salford.

The riots of 1981 left other non-physical legacies, such as setting a precedent for future tense episodes against the government. They also proved that if you create enough damage, the issue at hand can be at least talked about. However, most governments and ministers pay lip service to caring about the issues.

The anger of the people was obviously going to spill into the stands at football matches. Attending wasn't fun for many during the 70s and 80s. The stadiums were falling apart, toilets were old, and probably only for men. The food was horrible and fans were put into pens. Stadium disasters were happening up and down the country. At the time, you had the second Ibrox disaster, and the hooligan firms were becoming really bad. Crowds were often lacking basic manners and were full of aggression, and that's before the battle between the rival fans. Because it was mostly a masculine crowd, the environment had an air of an all-boys school. With that mass grouping of men, there was a heady odour of sweat, tobacco, booze and unhealthy food. Trying to get into position on the terrace was generally hazardous. If the balance of play shifted, there was a rush of bodies pushing you forwards. You could be pushed against a barrier, down steps or against people. Many injuries occurred, but it was often looked upon as a badge of honour.

The terraces were a cheap way to watch the match, but you had to know what you were getting into, and hold your own. The march to the match, while a great way to be with friends and get into the spirit of things, was also another choke point for hooliganism. There was a mixture of touts, souvenir sellers and food trolleys up and down whichever ground you were heading to. The food was unhealthy, and it's hard to imagine how more people didn't fall ill to food poisoning.

Football programmes were in their infancy at the time. There were programmes such as *Jack Heller's Hammer*, *Albert Sewell's Chelsea*, or the ones at West Bromwich Albion, Coventry City and Derby County. Clubs made an effort, but the programmes were a prehistoric version of what we see today – the typical notes from the manager, profiles of the opposition, results, etc. Then there was the fanzine culture that was beginning to pop up at this time. They were from working-class roots and were a form of self-created rebellion against the hostile environment for football fans. What predominated the backdrop of the sport at the time were also dodgy dealings and unique financial interests, providing a form of expression away from the established narrative. This new form of written word took off, creating a popular subculture. Fanzines come and go, and many times there's more than one at a club. They talked about political and social issues that affected football, but there was also music, fashion, comedy and art in its many forms. The overall feel of fanzines is like the punk genre of the 70s. But first and foremost they were a way to show that all fans weren't thugs. Created before the internet, there wasn't the access to information, outside of a local paper, so these filled the void for a while. There are still some fanzines around from those days, one such being *The City Gent*, which came on the scene in 1984.

For the time, the turnstiles were in poor shape. They were rickety, rusting and offered little security. The stadium started to fill up on a Saturday by 2pm for a 3pm kick-off. At that time it was so ingrained into the public that even most non-fans knew what time the match started. For the uninitiated, the reason behind the 3pm kick-off was due to the Factory Act, introduced in 1850. The law was to improve workers' rights and was passed to prevent companies keeping employees any later than 2pm on Saturdays. Churches were concerned that workers would turn to drink and spend their time at a pub, so they wanted people to spend their time in other pursuits, such as setting up football clubs. The 3pm kick-off was considered to provide enough time for workers to clock off and get to the match, as there wasn't good transportation then. People basically had to walk, and with very few other things to do, it was football for them. As the sport gained popularity, the professional leagues popped up. Matches also needed to finish by sundown, as floodlights didn't appear until the 50s. Weekday fixtures weren't unusual, but getting away from work and there being no floodlights caused problems.

Then came the 60s, when the blackout rule was put into effect. Burnley's chairman Bob Lord was concerned that match attendances would drop if the fixtures were on television. He convinced other clubs that it would be detrimental, so the FA introduced the blackout rule. The rule stipulated that any match in the professional leagues that kicked off on a Saturday at 3pm wasn't allowed to be aired.

One of the few good things to come out of the Covid pandemic recently was the blackout rule being dropped for a season. In 2020/21 the FA dropped the rule, since stadiums were empty due to stay-at-home regulations. For the first time in over 40 years, matches were broadcast live at 3pm on Saturday TV.

Pre-match rituals at the time weren't anything like they are today. At the most the teams would come out on to the pitch five minutes before kick-off, shoot at a keeper and maybe do some sprints. The supporters would chant the name of a player as they warmed up, to which said player would wave back or give a thumbs-up. One could feel closer to the players than now. Players generally mixed with supporters, either in town or spent time talking to fans. There were fewer opportunities for TV appearances, and little space for interviews, since there was less media at the time.

The away fans would be met with a chant of 'you'll never make the station'. Most of the matches had hooliganism and fights. Before the football officials figured out segregation, home fans would infiltrate the away end to start a fight, especially if the home team was losing. The away fans, if they were bold, would try to take the home end, sectioning them off with a wall. Sight lines were poor if you were at one end of the stadium. If the goal went in at the other end, you could easily miss it.

Pitch invasions were a sporadic occurrence in the 70s and 80s. On 13 May 1989, at a match between Crystal Palace and Birmingham City, there was a big rush between the two sets of fans. This happened not long after Hillsborough. Birmingham City fans included the Zulu Warriors, a firm that became very famous in the late 80s. The pitch was invaded a couple of times during a match that Palace won 4-1, with a hat-trick from Ian Wright. There were 16 people arrested, and one person was stabbed. The papers described it as a

'Brawl at Palace'. This was one of the many reasons the Thatcher government wanted to introduce identification for the fans.

The game of football was much slower at the time. Managers would sit in the dugout, on top of the stand or in the directors' box, with little touchline theatrics. It was more about the team and the players, but the cult of the manager was beginning to arrive in the 70s with the likes of Malcolm Allison, Brian Clough and Don Revie. The sport was tougher, but was also full of skilful mavericks who were moving with the times. These mavericks were very similar to the star players nowadays, sometimes unreliable, sometimes playing for themselves, but they were exciting. Most of them from this generation didn't make the England team or gained very few caps.

One of the things in many stadiums that has unfortunately continued to today is that, at half-time, music is blasted from a sound system. It might be part of the plan to drive fans into the bowels of the stadium to buy overpriced food or to talk about the match. In the 70s the half-time scores of other matches were put on a manual scoreboard. Usually there was a staff member who would place the numbers on the board, and a man with a transistor radio would also inform the fans around him of the scores. Nowadays the sport runs rings around the past, as the information flow and media connectivity is first-rate. Everyone in the stadium has a device in their pocket. In 1976, unless you were close to that man with the radio, you had to wait until you got home for the final scores. If the match was on a Saturday, you had to find a newspaper agent selling an evening paper such as the *London Evening Standard* or the *Evening News*. These ran classified editions with the results, first-half reports and summaries with league tables. The other big bit of news you would get out of the reports was which fixtures were being featured on TV over the weekend.

So you've gone to the match, suffered some awful conditions and now you have to get out. That's where it got tricky, as you needed to get out of the ground and away before the visiting fans were released from their pen. Once you got out, you had to deal with the police, who didn't treat the supporters well. But once you were on your way, you were fine.

Hooliganism has largely gone from the game now, but will never be stamped out completely. However, some of the passion has been sapped out of the grounds in order to provide safe matches. Most crowds are looking for the action on the pitch for their spark. The people who used to create the atmosphere of those times are older now, but that experience has seen attendances plummet. However, these hooligan firms weren't just started in the 60s. It goes all the way back to the late 19th century. Whatever term you want to use for it, the fans were causing not just trouble in the stands but on the pitch too. The sport had come from the working classes in Britain, and this hooliganism was its links with the past. During the inter-war years, the sport became slightly more respectable, but levels of disorder and public concern were around. So, in this context, football grounds were public spaces for large-scale threatening ritual displays.

This is when gangs and firms started kicking up within football grounds, staking claim to their territory. Tribal loyalties, with a gang-like mentality. These types of actions are widely accepted as the principal reason behind particular rivalries in the sport. Violence has created some of that, plus regional factors such as sectarianism in Glasgow. Until the Taylor Report, football violence was confined to the football grounds. Now any place near the stadium is ripe for violence. The game brings to the surface emotions in people who usually wouldn't act the same way outside of the sport. It's both positive and negative; if something good happens during a match, the positivity comes out, but if it's something bad, well, we've seen the destruction.

The hooliganism of the 70s also spread to the continent. At the 1974 UEFA Cup Final between Feyenoord and Tottenham Hotspur, Spurs fans created a lot of damage before rampaging through the streets of Rotterdam. This was one of the major reasons why Bill Nicholson walked away from White Hart Lane a few months later. The following season, Leeds fans at the European Cup Final in Paris threw things on to the pitch and laid destruction to the streets after the match.

The start of the problems in the 1970s can be linked back to the British far right, and 1967 is a good place to start the discussion. This was when the National Front was formed. It was the first time since Oswald Moseley's British Union of Fascists that far-right groups came together under one banner. The National Front was insignificant by the 2020s, but was a major player in 1977. It won a quarter of a million votes in the Greater London Council elections; then 33 years later the British National Party put up 338 candidates and amassed a half a million votes in the 2010 general election.

You're faced with a lot of ideology that has been debunked, or so-called facts that have been proven to be wrong. The National Front did go after the Jewish significantly, even producing books trying to prove their points. So many people just brushed off these views as stupid or crazy, without seeing the danger behind them. The peaks and troughs in the movement miss the point: the movement had the ability to incite hatred and undermine the free thought of society.

On 1 June 1981 a group of Black youths gathered at Melfort Park for an attack on the Wilton Arms, which was seen as the centre of National Front activity. The pub was stormed and a leader of the local football firm, a National Front member, was injured. While the group kept moving down the street, an innocent bystander, Terence May, a White teenager, was pulled from his vehicle and killed. After this riot, 15 Black youths and men were arrested on offences from riotous assembly to murder.

In football, the period between 1978 and 1981 was dominated in England by Nottingham Forest, Ipswich

Town and Aston Villa on their triumphs through Europe. And, of course, Liverpool were always around at the top of the game. Crystal Palace, on the other hand, although very much in the mind of local supporters and television chat shows, lacked silverware. This lack of success has always kept them on the outer rim of the football radar. The occasional cup final appearance, yo-yoing through the divisions, and some outstanding players, including Kenny Sansom and Ian Wright, has made them fun to watch. The late 70s to the early 80s cemented the club in the mind of 'exotic' fans.

Chapter 3

1979/80 – the Eagles Flying High

FOR A brief moment in time Crystal Palace sat top of the First Division. This was at the beginning of 1979/80. The great Liverpool team of the mid-70s was ageing and many of their players would be off to other clubs by the end of the season. They had started the league season poorly, with two wins, three draws and two defeats. However, they recovered to win the league for the fourth time in five seasons. Meanwhile, Nottingham Forest became back-to-back European Cup champions. So, for Palace to sit at the top, even for one night, was some achievement, and the first time in the club's history.

It was achieved with a 4-1 win over Ipswich on Saturday, 29 September. Coming into the match the Tractor Boys were in good form, so would be no pushover. David Swindlehurst opened the scoring for Palace with a stunning volley after 17 minutes. Paul Hinshelwood made it two just before the half-hour mark, then Gerry Francis scored from the spot just before the break. Eric Gates pulled one back for Ipswich on the stroke of half-time to give his team some hope, but this was quashed when Jim Cannon fired home Palace's fourth.

Ipswich were a well-run and successful club, managed by future England manager Bobby Robson, but this day was all about Terry Venables's team, which had achieved promotion to the top tier only the season before. Players such as Cannon, Swindlehurst and Hinshelwood were complemented by five players from the FA Youth Cup-winning team of 1977: Kenny Samson, Peter Nicholas, Billy Gilbert, Jerry Murphy and Vince Hilaire. Venables had brought in Mike Flanagan from Charlton Athletic and former England captain Gerry Francis from QPR.

The opening match of 1979/80 saw Crystal Palace travel to Manchester City, managed by Malcolm Allison, who had led Palace for three years earlier in the decade, following a previous stint at City. It ended goalless, as did Palace's next match, at home to Southampton. There was then a third consecutive draw, away at Middlesbrough, 1-1, before Palace's first win of the season, beating Derby 4-0. Against a Derby team that included Roy McFarland, Dave Webb, Gordon Hill, Gerry Daly and Bruce Rioch, Palace's goals came from Nicholas, Swindlehurst and a brace from new signing Flanagan. A couple of years earlier, Flanagan, while on loan from Charlton to the New England Tea Men in the US, had scored 30 times in 28 matches to win the league's Most Valuable Player award over the likes of Giorgio Chinaglia, Trevor Francis and Franz Beckenbauer.

In the League Cup second round, Palace thrashed Stockport 7-0 with goals from Hilaire, Murphy, Francis and two for both Flanagan and Walsh, to give them an 8-1 aggregate victory. However, the flow of goals then dried up when Palace went to Wolves and came away with a 1-1 draw. After further victories, 2-0 against Aston Villa, 2-1 against Stoke, followed by the Ipswich result, Palace were one of only two clubs unbeaten in the Football League, the other being Fourth Division Walsall. However, Palace had suffered a defeat to Wolves, which saw them exit the League Cup in the third round.

The excitement of Palace's early season league form meant that more than 45,000 fans packed into Selhurst Park for the visit of Spurs. Ian Walsh scored in his first match of the season in the 1-1 draw. The result dropped Palace to third as Manchester United and Forest moved into the top two places. At the time, no one knew this would start a downward spiral for Palace. It started with the first league defeat of the season, which came at The Dell against Southampton. Paul Hinshelwood scored for Palace, but a hat-trick from Phil Boyer contributed to the Saints' 4-1 victory. Things went from bad to worse on a trip to Goodison Park to play Everton, where Palace were beaten 3-1. The Eagles had slipped to fifth in the table, but the rot was partially stopped with successive 1-1 draws, against Bristol City and Bolton, who would both be relegated at the end of the season.

Palace returned to winning ways at the start of November, beating Manchester City 2-0 and Arsenal

1-0, with Swindlehurst scoring in both matches. He was then on target again in an impressive 1-1 draw at Old Trafford against high-flying Manchester United, to move the Eagles up to third in the table, just one point behind Liverpool and United.

Over the next five matches Palace scored only one goal. This came at Selhurst Park in a 1-0 victory over European Cup holders Nottingham Forest, via Ian Walsh. During this goal drought, the Eagles drew 0-0 with Coventry, lost 1-0 to Leeds, and 3-0 to Liverpool and to Brighton. The trip to Anfield on 15 December was key, as the reigning league champions were just three points ahead of Palace. However, goals by Jimmy Case, Kenny Dalglish and Terry McDermott showed the gulf in class. The crushing defeat to rivals Brighton, struggling near the foot of the table, saw Palace drop three places, so Boxing Day saw them in eighth place, still unbeaten at home, but with only one away victory in 11 matches on the road.

That unbeaten home record didn't last long, as 1979 ended with a 2-1 defeat by Middlesbrough at Selhurst Park. It was a sad end to a year that had promised so much just three months earlier. The new year did at least bring a point, a goalless draw at home to Norwich, before the Eagles entered the FA Cup in the third round. They were drawn away to Second Division Swansea City. The two clubs hadn't met in 15 years but would now meet three times in ten days. At the Vetch, two John Toshack goals for the Swans cancelled out goals by Kember and

Walsh for the Eagles, then the replay ended 3-3 after extra time. The second replay, in Cardiff, saw the Swans victorious, 2-1, to end any cup dreams for Eagles fans. Before the cup defeat, a return to league action saw two Walsh goals secure a 2-1 win over Derby. After the cup misery, Flanagan scored the only goal to beat Wolves, his first strike since October. Meanwhile, Swindlehurst was struggling to find the back of the net. His goal at Old Trafford in November was only his seventh of the season, but he had scored a third of Palace's goals so far. His lack of success coincided with Palace's struggles. Between the United match in November and the end of February, they scored only five times in 13 league matches, which contained only three victories.

While the rest of the First Division teams contested the fourth round of the FA Cup, Palace at least managed two goals in one match, although only drew 2-2 at home to West Brom. At this stage the Eagles were still flying relatively high in the league, in sixth place, but were only eight points ahead of their opponents in 18th. However, three successive defeats, to Aston Villa, Stoke and Ipswich, not scoring one goal, saw Palace down to tenth, only eight points above the relegation zone.

The pressure was eased slightly with a 1-1 draw with struggling Everton at Selhurst Park, before March commenced with a welcome victory, 2-0 at Bristol City. This was followed by a 3-1 home win over Bolton that saw Palace back up to seventh, well clear of the threat of relegation, and perhaps even with hopes of pushing for a European place. Only 18,728 had turned up at Selhurst Park for the Bolton match, which saw goals from Murphy and Hilaire to add to the opener by centre-back Billy Gilbert.

Sadly, this would be the last match in which Palace would score more than once for the remainder of the season. It was a run-in that saw them win only once in ten matches, 1-0 against Leeds. There was the consolation of a goalless draw against Liverpool, which saw the season's best home gate at Selhurst Park of 45,583, but Palace's poor form saw them finish 13th, a full 20 points behind champions Liverpool.

However, for a team that had been promoted the previous season, this was a respectable finish, if slightly disappointing given the way they had started the season. This should have been something to build on, and if Palace had, this book probably would have been written before. The lack of goals was their main problem, as they scored only 41 times in 42 league fixtures. Only relegated Bristol City and Bolton Wanderers scored fewer. This lack of goals sent the management team searching for a striker who would hopefully not cost too much. Little did they know that the player brought in would signal the downfall of this promising team.

Chapter 4

The 1970s – When the Eagles Finally Soared

PALACE MANAGER Terry Venables was just 36 at the start of the 1979/80 season, very young for someone in this role, but he had proved his quality in getting Palace into the top tier and taking them to the top of the table, if only briefly. On 11 May 1979, the day before Arsenal's dramatic last-minute victory over Manchester United in the FA Cup Final, Palace played Burnley. Win and Palace were champions, draw and they would be promoted behind rivals Brighton. Lose and they would miss out completely. The attendance was 51,801, still the highest in the club's history. Palace won 2-0 to become Second Division champions.

This wasn't the first time Crystal Palace reached the top tier. Promotion was achieved ten years earlier in 1968/69 under Bert Head, who took them into the First Division for the first time in their history. They survived by the skin of their teeth the following season, just one point above the drop, but improved to 18th in 1970/71. They struggled again in 1971/72, finishing one place above the relegation zone, before the inevitable drop came the following season.

On 17 February 1973, Palace beat fellow strugglers Stoke City 3-2 at Selhurst Park, thanks to goals by Derek Possee, Alan Whittle and Don Rogers. They were in 17th place but it was tight at the bottom of the table, with only four points separating the teams in 14th and 21st. Palace were still only one point above the teams in the relegation places. Two draws and four defeats saw them drop to 20th, where they remained despite a 2-0 victory over Chelsea at Selhurst Park. Defeats to Sheffield United and Manchester United saw the Eagles fall into the bottom two, where they would finish, two points from safety.

Meanwhile, Bert Head had been moved upstairs, with the flamboyant Malcolm Allison put in charge of the team. Back in the mid-1970s the main image formed of Allison was of a big man in a sheepskin coat, wearing a wide-brimmed fedora. He couldn't save Palace from relegation. Even worse, they were relegated to the Third Division in his first full season in charge. Most managers would have been sacked after two straight relegations but the board liked what 'Big Mal' brought to Selhurst Park and believed he had a sound tactical mind.

Although Palace didn't bounce straight back in 1974/75, they had a good season and finished fifth in the table. They repeated this in 1975/76, but reached the semi-final of the FA Cup, having beaten Leeds, Chelsea and Sunderland on the way. They lost to eventual winners Southampton, but failure to gain promotion led Allison to resign at the end of the season, although it wouldn't be the last Palace heard of him.

In came Venables, another character of the game, as well as being a singer and successful writer. He had been given a coaching role at the club by Allison after having retired from playing through injury, so it was a natural progression. Venables had helped mould the team in the Third Division, but also nurtured young players, which led to Palace winning the FA Youth Cup in successive seasons, 1976/77 and 1977/78. Only Manchester United and Chelsea had previously achieved this feat. Most of these youth players eventually made it into the Palace first team as they moved up the divisions over the coming years. The Eagles made it out of the Third Division in 1976/77, finishing third, but they didn't start to gel until the following season, finishing a creditable ninth in the Second Division.

The following season saw the Eagles soaring to the top of the Second Division, gaining promotion back to the top tier at last. The season commenced well for Palace, who hit top spot early in October 1978 after a 3-1 win over arch-rivals Brighton, leaving the Eagles unbeaten after nine matches. They extended this run by two further matches before finally tasting defeat, at home to Fulham, who were also challenging at the top of the table. This was quickly followed by a second consecutive defeat, this time at Burnley, to dampen Palace fans' hopes of a return to the big time.

However, they got back to winning ways and the top of the table during November, where they stayed until early February, when Brighton took over top spot, although the Eagles had a match in hand. This period also saw Palace take the scalp of First Division Middlesbrough in the FA Cup, with a rare Kenny Sansom goal giving them victory in the home replay after a 1-1 draw at Ayresome Park. They followed this up in the fourth round by defeating another First Division club, Bristol City, with a resounding 3-0 scoreline at Selhurst Park, showing that if they could maintain their league form, they wouldn't be out of place in the top tier next season. However, their promising cup run came to an end with a 1-0 home defeat to Wolves, another First Division club. Meanwhile, other results in the league saw Palace drop to fourth, out of the promotion spots.

From March, Palace just had the league to focus on and started the month with a 1-0 home win over Wrexham, which moved them back up to third in the table. By the end of the month they were up to second, chasing Brighton, two points adrift but with two matches in hand due to their long FA Cup run. However, by the time Palace had played those matches, a poor run left them a point adrift of the Seagulls in what looked like a four-horse race for the title and the three promotion places, along with Stoke and Sunderland.

With just three matches remaining, Brighton, Stoke and Palace sat on 51 points, with Sunderland just two points behind them, but with a match in hand, so it was all to play for. On 21 April, Brighton drew, so Stoke's victory took them top. Palace had no match, so Sunderland's victory at Cambridge took them into third place. Then Sunderland hit top spot with a resounding 6-2 victory over Sheffield United, although a Palace success in their match in hand would take them top.

Brighton and Palace both won on 28 April but Stoke only drew and Sunderland suffered a shock 2-1 defeat at home to lowly Cardiff City. Brighton led the league again, but Palace were still to play their crucial match in hand. The final matches of the season for Palace's rivals came on 5 May, and they all won. Therefore Palace's 1-0 win at Orient on the same day left them in fourth place for now, level on points with Sunderland and one point behind Brighton and Stoke. However, an inferior goal difference meant they needed to win their final match to become champions, while a draw would see them finish third, but still achieve promotion.

Six days later came the match at home to Burnley that saw the 2-0 victory in front of over 50,000 people, way higher than any of the three First Division matches that day. The gates were closed an hour before kick-off. Burnley held out well and a draw looked inevitable until, with just 14 minutes remaining, Ian Walsh headed home Vince Hilaire's cross to send the Palace fans wild. Cue a pitch invasion. Soon after the pitch was cleared,

Dave Swindlehurst settled things by adding a second for Palace to clinch the league title by just one point from Brighton and Stoke. Cue another pitch invasion, but the fans had something to celebrate: Palace were back in the First Division, to challenge the likes of Liverpool, who had won the league yet again.

* * *

You've already read how Palace's first season back in the top tier went. Early promise, followed by the mediocrity of mid-table. The fans were looking forward to the next season but, of course, summer transfer windows are generally where most of the business is done in preparation for the upcoming campaign. Palace signed young goalkeeper Paul Barron from Arsenal, along with Clive Allen, who had moved there from QPR but didn't play a competitive match for the Gunners. Going the other way was Kenny Sansom, one of the major players in Palace's successful rise. Allen had been a prolific goalscorer for QPR, so it was hoped that he would resolve Palace's shortage of goals from the previous season.

The 1980/81 season could hardly have started with a tougher match, away at champions Liverpool, with Barron between the posts, and Flanagan and Allen up top. Palace proved no match for Liverpool, who swept them aside 3-0. In fact, Palace were involved in some high-scoring encounters early in the season, losing their next match 4-3 at home to Spurs, before gaining their first points of the season in a 5-2 victory over Middlesbrough, with Allen hitting a hat-trick. Meanwhile, Palace progressed to the third round of the League Cup with a two-legged victory over Bolton.

There was controversy in Palace's next league match against Coventry when Allen took a free kick from outside the area. The ball went into the goal, hit the stanchion and bounced out. No VAR or goal-line technology in those days, and both the ref and linesman agreed that the ball had hit the post before coming back into play. The Eagles lost 3-1, one of six successive defeats that saw the goals dry up. It all looked very much like the season before.

The rot came to an end at Selhurst Park with a 2-1 victory over Leicester, with goals from Hilaire and Allen, but Palace were struggling, second from bottom, with only Manchester City below them. A victory in their next match, 3-2 against Southampton, saw a Flanagan hat-trick, and the hope that the goals may start to flow again, but the next three fixtures brought just two goals, although one of those was in a single-goal victory over Manchester United. Despite a 2-2 draw at home to Liverpool on 15 November the Eagles had hit the bottom of the table and never recovered. By this time Venables had left the club to join Second Division QPR, for reasons that have never been made clear. Ernie Walley took over as caretaker for six matches, before the return of Malcolm Allison.

The only highlights of the remainder of the season were a 4-1 victory over Norwich in which Allen scored two more goals, and a 3-1 win over Birmingham. However, by the time of the latter, in April 1981, Palace were nine points adrift at the bottom and 11 points from safety. They ended a full 13 points behind Leicester City, who were also relegated, along with Norwich City. Palace won just six league matches during the season, all at Selhurst Park, although they managed to score six more goals than the previous season. Clive Allen top-scored with nine goals.

The season was a different one for the game in England. Aston Villa were surprise winners of the league, and Ipswich Town were at one stage in the hunt for a treble of league, FA Cup and UEFA Cup, but only succeeded in the latter. It's interesting to note that Aston Villa weren't big spenders and used only 14 players all season, proving the old mantra that money isn't a guarantee of winning in the top flight. They didn't concede many goals, and scored plenty, with Peter Withe hitting 20. Meanwhile, Liverpool won the European Cup, and Tottenham won the FA Cup. However, the football establishment was becoming worried about high ticket prices in a time of recession, plus too much TV coverage of matches. Why weren't the fans going to matches? Maybe it was obvious.

At the end of the season further big moves were made at Palace. Big Mal was off again after failing to save them from relegation, while Clive Allen left to join old boss Terry Venables at QPR. Palace had now gone from what looked like being the team of the 80s, at one time sitting top of the First Division, to being back in the second tier, having sold their leading goalscorer.

Chapter 5

Malcolm Allison – the Early Years

HE WAS a character, but Malcolm Allison first and
foremost wanted to win, with style. Manchester City saw
that. While there, Malcolm wanted to develop a team
like the Busby Babes, but had to wait until he arrived in
London to attempt this. Unlike the Manchester United
manager, Big Mal didn't get to see out the end of his
project at Crystal Palace.

Jon Spurling's book *Get It On: How the '70s Rocked
Football* talks a lot about Allison. In fact, the greater the
'Big Mal' caricature became, the more his footballing
powers waned. 'By then, Malcolm thought he was bigger
than the game, but no one is,' argued Alan Hudson.
In the brief period between Allison departing Maine
Road and taking over as Crystal Palace manager, Terry
O'Neill captured the essence of Big Mal perfectly in
his 1973 portrait, which shows Allison with his shirt
completely unbuttoned, wearing an enormous, intricately
carved medallion around his neck that wouldn't have
looked out of place on one of the Bee Gees. Terry O'Neill

memorably described Allison's turbulent three-year spell at Selhurst Park to me as a 'blur of skirt-chasing, fedora-wearing, cigar-chomping, publicity-grabbing ridiculousness'.

There was more to Malcolm Allison than his public persona. He was born in Dartford in 1927 and started his playing career at Charlton Athletic just after the war, although he made just two first-team appearances in his six years there. He was at Charlton during one of their most successful periods, under Jimmy Seed, assisted by his good friend Jimmy Trotter. After rising through the leagues, Charlton were one of the most consistent teams in the top flight before the Second World War stopped their progress. They reached the FA Cup Final in 1946, losing to Derby County, but went one better the following year when defeating Burnley 1-0 in the final.

However, Allison wasn't part of this success and let the management team at Charlton know that he wasn't impressed with the training or coaching at The Valley. He moved to West Ham in 1951, playing under Ted Fenton. Fenton was responsible for developing the 'Academy of Football' and the 'West Ham Way' of playing. Always the eager pupil, Allison took on the training of some of the younger players, including Bobby Moore.

Fenton was a believer in homegrown talent, and developing them into the best players. The academy focused on two things: bringing skilful players in and ensuring they played the passing game on the pitch. Great players such as World Cup winners Bobby Moore,

Geoff Hurst and Martin Peters all emerged from this background. Taking advantage of what he learned in his coaching role at West Ham as his playing career was running down, Allison would later use this knowledge at Manchester City and Crystal Palace.

In 1957 Allison contracted tuberculosis, which led to him losing a lung. Having made 238 appearances for West Ham's first team, he came back to play for the reserves, and later played for non-league Romford. However, he never fully regained his fitness and was forced to retire in 1962. At first he looked for work outside the sport. He tried his luck as a second-hand car salesman, a gambler and a nightclub owner, but eventually returned to football. His first job as a coach was at Cambridge University, before moving on to manage non-league Bath City, where he discovered Tony Book, a future Manchester City legend. While at Bath, Allison took them into the third round of the FA Cup, only to lose to Bolton after a replay.

After spells at Toronto City and Plymouth Argyle, Allison became assistant to Joe Mercer at Manchester City in 1965, during what was then one of the club's most successful periods. The players they brought through the ranks are some of the best in England's history, such as Colin Bell, Mike Summerbee and Francis Lee. City played an exciting, fast-flowing brand of football that delighted all but their bitter rivals.

During this time City won the First Division in 1967/68, so entered the European Cup the following season. Big Mal was good with his quotes, saying that this City team would frighten the clubs in Europe. This was at a time when the Soviet Union had invaded Czechoslovakia, which led to UEFA pairing many of the Eastern Bloc countries against each other in the early rounds. Some of the clubs decided to withdraw from the competition in protest. However, in the first round City faced Fenerbahçe of Turkey and were beaten 2-1 on aggregate. They did, though, have cup success, winning the FA Cup in 1969, before doubling up with the League Cup and European Cup Winners' Cup in 1970. They also saw a doubling of attendances for home fixtures.

After this, some political games started in the backroom, which ended up derailing a very good team. When new chairman Peter Swales came in, he wanted Allison as sole manager, but Joe Mercer refused to stand down. Mercer was very different to Big Mal, more like a father figure to his players, while Allison was the tactical brain, but loud and brash with it. He was also the guy who had the players training like athletes, making them run on machines. And it was Allison who won the power struggle in the end, as Mercer moved on, leaving Big Mal in charge.

However, City's previous success didn't last, and neither did Malcolm Allison. Although they won the Charity Shield during his sole tenure, in 1972/73 they were struggling in mid-table, and Allison had resigned by March 1973. He walked straight into the manager's role at Crystal Palace, failing to save them from relegation from the top flight, as we've already seen.

On arrival at Selhurst Park, Big Mal began to make huge changes, from the bottom up. The old Aston Villa-inspired claret and blue was gone, replaced by the current red and blue stripes, although this is something the club disputes, saying that these colours were from 1937/38, and may even have been used in Croydon during the 1908 season. The old badge was replaced by a Benfica-inspired eagle, and Allison also replaced the nickname of 'The Glaziers' with 'The Eagles'. The original nickname was a reference to the club's association with the Crystal Palace. In the early years of the club, they were referred to in the local papers as 'The Crystals', before the name was changed to 'The Glaziers' around 1910.

But for all the work Allison did off the pitch, on it the performances were miserable, as in 1973/74 they succumbed to the drop for the second successive season. One player identified by Allison during this time, though, was Peter Taylor, who turned out to be a great player during Palace's subsequent ascent up the divisions. On why he needed Peter Taylor in the team, Mal said:

> I always wanted to play a left-winger in the outside-right position or a right-sided player outside-left. When I saw Peter Taylor play I knew I was going to sign him. I was going to make him my outside-right and he destroyed full-backs, destroyed teams. He was exceptional

down that right-hand side. He used to bring the house down. The crowd used to go berserk.

Once again, Malcolm Allison was a man ahead of his time, as now we see the inverted-winger system used by most teams.

I interviewed Jim Piddock, a Hollywood actor, long-time Palace fan and creator of the Crystal Palace Supporters' Trust. We talked about the club, Malcolm Allison and everything around that era of Crystal Palace. Our email chat started about what people originally thought of Malcolm when he came in: 'I think the players and fans all bought into the arrival of Malcolm Allison because of his reputation as a top-level coach. But the truth is he was far more important in terms of raising the media profile of the club in a marketing way than in any football-related manner.'

Allison was thought of very highly because of his success at Manchester City, but of course that success was also down to Joe Mercer. Once he didn't have Mercer, Allison had been shown to be all bark and no bite. What he did try to do, though, was find his Joe Mercer with Terry Venables. Although Allison's two stints with Palace were very disappointing, they did at least lead to better times under Venables. It's sad, however, that Allison came in with such high expectations based on his reputation. As Jim said, 'We'd been relegated from Division One the season before and expectations were very high when he arrived, but the reality was that the football side of things was severely lacking. We lost our first game of the season 4-1 at home and things got worse from there.'

The Eagles returned to the Third Division for the first time in 11 years for 1974/75. Allison made pivotal moves that secured his legacy after he left: from QPR came Terry Venables, and Ian Evans came in an exchange for Don Rogers. Allison also convinced the board to invest heavily at youth level, which in turn led to the development of the famous Crystal Palace academy that would be the backbone of the Team of the 80s. By 1975, Venables's body finally told him to give up playing, due to arthritis, so Allison added him to the coaching staff.

A few years later, in an official Crystal Palace team publication when the club were promoted to the First Division in 1978/79, England Manager Ron Greenwood heaped praise on the team:

> The highest accolade that I can pay Crystal Palace and its players is that I compare them with the Busby Babes of the 1950s. Their youth policy has been proven. It has produced the young players who are now making up half the side which won promotion for the Club. There is a host of others knocking at the door too and from a football point of view, the whole future looks very rosy for Terry Venables and his Crystal Palace youngsters. I also feel that great credit has got to be given to the Board of Directors.

Greenwood, while an interesting figure in the sport, was from that West Ham United system that helped Allison grow as a person and a coach. So it's not too strange to see him compliment a team that played with Palace's style under Venables.

Big Mal did have his good points at this time as well. His charisma, coaching ability and rebranding of the club was a positive in the longer term. Peter Taylor, before Big Mal spotted him, was struggling for his place at Third Division Southend United, but three years later was in the England team. According to Taylor, Allison had tried to sign him four times while he was at Manchester City, as well as previously at Palace.

For all the radical stuff Allison is linked with, his tactical nous was first class. He used the flexible back-five system during the mid-1970s at a declining Third Division club that needed a kick up the backside. His defence was made up of the back three, which became a back five when defending. This allowed the midfield to be made up of two defensive and three offensive players, the two defensive midfielders operating as wing-backs. In the English game this was again ahead of its time.

With Palace deemed too good for the Third Division, expectations for 1974/75 were high. This was also a season when the seeds were sown for the rivalry with Brighton & Hove Albion, commencing on Saturday, 17 August at the Goldstone Ground in front of over 26,000 fans. This was the first match in charge of Brighton for another Peter Taylor, Brian Clough's old right-hand man. While Clough had moved on to Leeds, Taylor remained at Brighton in sole charge. With such a large gathering, inevitably it resulted in violence, with 85 police officers, dogs, motorbikes and horses in place to control the crowd. There were 20 arrests as fights broke out between the fans.

Big Mal came into the match in charge of a team deemed one of the favourites for promotion, and was right to think that Brighton were a step below them. However, Taylor had other plans, and his team ground out a 1-0 win, with Palace guilty of missing good chances through Mick Hill, Alan Whittle and Don Rogers. They did have the ball in the back of the net in the 37th minute but it was ruled out. Alan Whittle headed the ball against the bar, the rebound falling to Mel Blyth, who slotted home. At first glance there seemed to be nothing wrong with the goal, but Blyth was flagged offside. Brighton's winner came from the left foot of debutant Ian Mellor.

Palace didn't have much time to regroup, as their League Cup campaign kicked off just four days later at Vicarage Road against Watford. This wasn't yet the Watford of the Graham Taylor/Sir Elton John era, with Palace's opponents also in the Third Division. It ended in a 1-1 draw, thus adding another match to the busy start to the season. However, before the replay, Palace returned to league action, at Selhurst Park against Tranmere. It was a routine 2-1 win for Palace, with goals from Blyth and Swindlehurst. Three days later, Palace showed their dominance in beating Watford 5-1 in the League Cup replay, with a brace from Whittle adding to goals from Taylor, Chatterton and an own goal. The Eagles were drawn to play Second Division Bristol City in the next round. To finish the first month of the season, Palace journeyed to Halifax Town, where they were soundly beaten 3-1. A poor start to the league season saw Palace in 21st place after three matches.

On a very rainy 7 September at Selhurst Park, Palace hit top form, defeating Swindon Town 6-2, Whittle and Swindlehurst both scoring twice. This moved them up to a more respectable ninth in the table, but they were soon brought back down to earth when they were dumped out of the League Cup, losing 4-1 at home to Bristol City three days later. However, their league form continued to improve as they gained their first away victory of the season on a trip to Roots Hall, where they beat table-toppers Southend United 1-0 thanks to Chatterton's goal. Palace stayed on the road for their next match, at Edgar Street against Hereford United, but unfortunately their recent good run came to an end in a 2-0 defeat, leaving them in mid-table.

League fixtures were still coming fast and furious, with Palace back in action four days later, defeating Wrexham 2-0 at Selhurst Park. Then just three days on they won again at home, this time 1-0 against Preston, who were top of the table and managed by one Bobby Charlton. Palace moved up to fourth after this victory, and finished off September with a third successive win, this time 1-0 at Huddersfield, moving the Eagles up another place, just two points off the top of the table.

The start of October saw Grimsby visit Selhurst Park, where they were soundly beaten 3-0. Palace were now playing confidently and sat top of the table, where most had expected them to be when the season commenced. However, this confidence was shattered on 5 October when mid-table Chesterfield came to Selhurst Park and went away with an unlikely 4-1 victory. It didn't get any better a week later either, when Palace went to Bournemouth and were despatched 4-0. After a run of four victories, Palace had now shipped eight goals in two matches and slipped to eighth in the table. They stopped this slide at home to Walsall with a 1-0 win, followed by another single-goal victory, this time against Blackburn Rovers, a third win against a team sitting top of the table. However, Palace's results against teams lower in the league weren't as impressive, and they finished October with a 2-1 defeat at mid-table Port Vale. Three months and 15 matches into the season, Palace were still in contention for promotion, though, sixth in the table, only three points behind leaders Preston in a closely fought contest.

November was a month of draws in the league. It started with a home 1-1 draw against fellow promotion contenders Peterborough United, before another 1-1, this time away at Blackburn, who were back at the top of the table. A third successive stalemate, 2-2 at Bury, still kept Palace in touch with the league leaders, before a 3-3 draw at home to Plymouth kept the record going. November eventually saw a victory, which came in the FA Cup first round, away at non-league Tooting & Mitcham, although it was a 2-1 struggle after falling behind at Sandy Lane, which saw a 10,000 gate. And the month ended with another success, as Palace finally got back to winning ways in the league, 2-1 against Charlton, in front of over 24,000 supporters. It was another good result against a strong team, which moved Palace back up to third, four points behind leaders Blackburn.

Now down to eighth, the new calendar year saw more home points dropped in a 2-2 draw with Hereford, before another victory over Watford, this time 1-0 at Selhurst Park. At this stage Palace were one of four teams on 31 points, all just three points behind Blackburn Rovers. Another big crowd, over 26,000, were at The Valley to watch second-placed Charlton see off Palace 1-0, before January ended with a 2-1 defeat at lowly Aldershot. Although the Eagles hadn't dropped off the pace at the top of the table, despite their poor results, they had now played two more matches than some of their challengers, so were in danger of missing out on the expected promotion.

February didn't start much better as a 2-2 home draw against Bury dropped Palace down to fifth place, another poor result against a team well below them in the table. Another two places and two points were dropped the following Saturday, although the 1-1 draw away at Peterborough was a creditable result against a team on the same points. Next came revenge for the recent defeat at Aldershot, this time Palace triumphing 3-0 on home soil. Goals from Swindlehurst, Taylor and Whittle gave them their most emphatic win for quite some time to keep them in the promotion hunt. It still seemed that Palace were saving their best performances for the top teams in the league as they next came away from second-placed Plymouth with a 1-0 victory, but then ended the month with a poor 1-1 draw at home to Halifax. However, the Eagles were still handily placed in fifth, just three points behind leaders Charlton.

March started with another decent 1-1 away draw, against Preston, but Blackburn were now edging away from them at the top, by four points but with a match in hand. And Rovers were to extend this lead the following week when they beat Tranmere, while Palace were drawing yet again, this time at home to Huddersfield, who were in the relegation places. At least came the satisfaction of a 3-0 home victory over Brighton, who were struggling in the lower reaches of the table, but a return to 1-1 draws in Palace's next match away at Swindon left them five points adrift of the top two, Blackburn and Charlton. Things did improve with a 2-1 home win over Colchester, although the long trip to North Wales to play Wrexham saw a goalless draw, which saw Palace in fourth place, still five points behind leaders Blackburn, with only seven matches left to play.

Although Palace had lost only once at home so far this season, they made it eight draws at the start of April, in a 1-1 stalemate with Port Vale. However, Blackburn only drew, and Charlton lost, so two of their title rivals failed to take advantage of Palace's failure to win. The only team to benefit was Plymouth, whose 2-1 defeat of Bury saw them move into second spot. Charlton won their next match, as did Plymouth, while Palace went down 2-1 at Grimsby, from the bottom half of the table. Plymouth now topped the table, seven points clear of the Eagles, although Blackburn would go top if they could at least draw their next match, which is exactly what they did.

Although Blackburn, Charlton and Plymouth all drew their next matches, Palace still managed to drop further behind as they lost 2-1 at mid-table Chesterfield. They also dropped behind Port Vale in the table, with promotion looking increasingly unlikely, although still mathematically possible. By the time Palace next played, Plymouth had won again, although on 19 April they dropped two points, while Charlton surprisingly lost at home. However, Blackburn achieved promotion with a 2-0 victory over Chesterfield. Palace, though, pulled off one of their better results, beating Bournemouth 4-1 at Selhurst Park. Finally, an emphatic result against a team at the other end of the table.

Two days after Derby County surprisingly won the First Division when Ipswich failed to win at Manchester City, Palace's hopes of promotion to the Second Division were dealt a fatal blow by a 3-0 defeat at Walsall. The next day, Blackburn were crowned Third Division champions after their emphatic 4-1 victory at Port Vale, while Plymouth ended their season on 59 points, despite defeat at Peterborough. Palace, meanwhile, were ten points adrift of the top two, down in seventh. Perhaps this realisation that all was lost released the shackles, as Palace stormed to a 4-0 home win over Gillingham in their penultimate fixture of the season, but then lost their last match 2-0 to relegated Tranmere, typifying their season.

A season that had promised much ended in a whimper, with Palace down in fifth but well adrift of the promoted Blackburn, Plymouth and Charlton. Surely next season would see Palace back in the second tier, wouldn't it?

Well, as you've already read they finished fifth again, but this would be a season when they so very nearly reached the FA Cup Final.

Before that, Palace commenced the season in the league with a 2-0 home win over Chester, before they entered the other domestic cup, the League Cup, with a 3-0 home success against Colchester United in the first leg. A second league victory, away at Chesterfield, saw Palace topping the table, before they suffered their first defeat of the season in the second leg of the League Cup; however, they scraped through 4-3 on aggregate. They then played Colchester for the third time this season, beating them 3-2 at Selhurst Park to maintain their 100 per cent league record. Things were looking good at this early stage for Allison's team.

September started where August left off, another victory, this time at Cardiff, before Palace went out of the League Cup after losing 2-1 at Fourth Division Doncaster. However, their league form continued with a 2-0 win over Rotherham, although their first points were then lost on the road at Walsall in a 1-1 draw. Normal service was resumed with a 4-2 win at Shrewsbury, to leave Palace four points clear at the top of the table. All good things must come to an end, but it had to be Brighton who inflicted Palace's first league defeat of the season, and it was at Selhurst Park, 1-0. This was followed by a home 1-1 draw against Sheffield Wednesday, which reduced Palace's lead at the top to just one point.

October saw a goalless draw at Port Vale, a 3-0 home success against Grimsby, another goalless draw, at Preston, a 2-2 draw at home to fellow high-flyers Hereford, and finally yet another draw, 1-1 at home to strugglers Southend. Despite only one victory in the month, Palace still led the table by a point, although the chasing pack had a match in hand.

It was back to winning ways at the start of November as the Eagles won 3-1 at Halifax and 2-1 at Swindon to open up a four-point lead. However, a 1-1 home draw against Peterborough halted momentum, albeit briefly as Palace then won at Wrexham 3-1 to move five points clear of second-placed Brighton.

Finally it was time for the FA Cup, where in the first round Palace looked to have a comfortable draw at home to Walton & Hersham of the Isthmian League. However, it was far from easy as Palace scraped to a 1-0 win to move into the second round. It was, though, much easier in their next league fixture, defeating Mansfield 4-1 at Selhurst Park. December then saw Palace move further ahead at the top with a single-goal victory at Bury, before the FA Cup returned two weeks before Christmas.

Palace had a tougher draw this time, away at fellow Third Division Millwall, where they drew 1-1, the Lions cancelling out Swindlehurst's goal late on to force a replay three days later. This time Palace made no mistake. Dave Kemp put them ahead, before Taylor doubled their lead before half-time. Although Millwall pulled a goal back in the second half, the Eagles went through to the third round, where teams from the top two divisions joined the fray.

Before Christmas it was back to league action, though, ironically at Millwall, where the Lions gained revenge for their cup exit by inflicting Palace's first away defeat in the league all season, 2-1. Palace then went down twice more before the end of the year, first at Aldershot, then at home to Gillingham, as their early season form began to desert them. However, they still led the table by five points from Brighton, although Hereford were only six points behind, with three matches in hand.

The start of the new year gave Palace the opportunity to put the poor run in the league behind them as they faced Northern Premier League Scarborough in the FA Cup third round. Big Mal turned up in his fedora, smoking a fat cigar, but Palace were far from superior to their non-league rivals in their 2-1 victory. However, they were too good for Colchester the following week, coming away from Layer Road with an emphatic 3-0 win to put their title hopes back on track. It was a great away win, but Palace's home form was a concern as they next drew 1-1 at Selhurst Park against Shrewsbury. They had now won only five of 13 matches at home in the league, drawing five and losing three.

In the fourth round of the FA Cup, Palace were handed a plum draw away at Leeds, currently second in the First Division. Having so far struggled against two non-league teams, few would have anticipated what was to come for the Eagles, but they marked tightly, tackled hard and chased down the opposition players, leaving them little time or space on the ball. Allison's plan was to push up on Duncan McKenzie and Allan Clarke, while negating the threat of Eddie Gray on the left. Lo and behold it worked. Along with their defensive tactics, winger Peter Taylor ran the Leeds defence ragged. Terry Yorath crashed into him in the 24th minute. Taylor got up and curled in a free kick for David Swindlehurst to rise, meeting the ball with his head, past goalkeeper David Harvey. It could have been a more comprehensive win for Palace, but Harvey was in world-class form. He got his hand to another free kick from Swindlehurst and also pushed away an Ian Evans header.

Meanwhile, Palace goalkeeper Paul Hammond had a quiet afternoon. Just after the hour mark he turned away a shot from Clarke, and Terry Yorath had a header cleared off the line by Peter Wall. Palace won 1-0 and joined the ranks of Colchester United, Sunderland and Bristol City as FA Cup giant killers of the mighty Leeds United.

Palace's next league fixture was a tough one, away at second-placed Hereford on 31 January. While a win would have stretched their lead at the top, it ended 1-1, but at least Hereford hadn't gained ground. However, they had played some of their matches in hand and were now only one point behind Palace, and had still played two fewer matches, so looked likely to take over the lead in the table.

Going into February, Palace were away at Rotherham United, where they were hammered 4-1, while Brighton were beating Millwall to move into second spot, just one point behind and with a match in hand. The following day Hereford won, which meant Palace were off the top for the first time this season. All three title contenders then drew their next matches, Palace again failing to win at home, drawing 3-3 with Swindon.

Next up for Palace was the distraction of the FA Cup, in which they now faced Chelsea, at the time struggling as a mid-table team in the Second Division. The match at Stamford Bridge saw Peter Taylor wreaking havoc once again, scoring twice to add to Chatterton's goal as Palace triumphed 3-2 to reach the quarter-finals. Things were also going their way in the league too, as Hereford and Brighton both suffered losses to leave the title race wide open. However, Palace failed to take advantage of this as they then lost 2-0 at Peterborough, who had now joined the fight at the top of the table.

The Eagles then slumped to fifth in the league after another disappointing home draw, 1-1 with Wrexham, while the other main protagonists in the chase all won. A key match then came against fellow promotion hopefuls Brighton at the Goldstone Ground. Over 33,000 saw the home team triumph 2-0 to further dent Palace's title challenge, and it seemed that their FA Cup run was having a detrimental impact on their league form. However, this changed in the next match as Palace finally got back to winning ways at Roots Hall against Southend, coming away with a 2-1 victory. Meanwhile, Hereford beat Peterborough 3-0 at London Road to move six points clear at the top of the table.

A week after Big Mal's old team Manchester City won the League Cup by defeating Newcastle United 2-1 at Wembley, Palace were back in FA Cup action against Second Division Sunderland, who had won the cup in 1973 after famously beating Leeds in the final. Sunderland were denied the chance to repeat their success, however, as a Whittle goal gave Palace the victory at Roker Park to send the Eagles soaring into the semi-finals. Again Palace's away form was excellent, in both cup and league, but their home form deserted them once more in a 2-2 draw with Port Vale, which meant they had drawn exactly half of their 16 home league fixtures. Thank goodness, then, for their away form, which saw them defeat Grimsby 2-1, Taylor scoring both goals. Hereford and Brighton both lost on the same day, so Palace were still certainly in the hunt for promotion, although Hereford had a healthy five-point lead and matches in hand, so looked odds-on for the title.

Palace's promotion hopes certainly brightened after a rare home victory, 2-0 over Preston, which saw the Eagles move into second place behind Hereford, two points ahead of Brighton. Taylor was again on the mark in a 1-1 draw at Mansfield, but wins for Brighton and Hereford saw Palace lose ground again. However, their two main rivals then played out a 1-1 draw while Palace were winning at home to Bury to regain that lost ground, before they let it slip again with a goalless draw at home to Millwall, who had now moved up to fourth in the table.

The FA Cup semi-finals on 3 April were played at neutral venues. While Manchester United played Derby County at Hillsborough, winning 2-0, Palace faced Second Division Southampton at Stamford Bridge, where the Eagles had already achieved one giant-killing in the cup by defeating Chelsea. Palace didn't play like underdogs; they went for the win against the Saints. Their defence looked sharp, with Ian Evans playing impressively, Jim Cannon playing with his normal fire and Alan Whittle looking sharp as an attacking option on the left of midfield. Peter Taylor, on the other hand, was carrying a knock and was constantly hit with hard tackles. However, Southampton, lacking a cutting edge, struggled to create chances, and it took until the final 15 minutes for the deadlock to be broken. The goal came from long range for Southampton, scored by Paul Gilchrist. Unfortunately, for Palace, the Saints then scored again after Cannon fouled Mick Channon and the referee pointed to the spot, although the foul looked to be outside the area. Up stepped David Peach to dash Crystal Palace's dream of playing in the final.

Even more unfortunately, Palace's league form fell completely apart following their FA Cup exit. Four days after defeat to the Saints, they lost away at Sheffield Wednesday 1-0, then three days after that lost 1-0 again, this time to Cardiff, now second in the table, at Selhurst Park. Palace were down in fifth place, eight points behind leaders Hereford but still only a couple of points below the promotion places, so it was all still to play for. However, the following week put paid to any realistic promotion hopes as Palace were held 1-1 at home by Halifax in midweek, with Taylor missing a crucial penalty.

Sadly, fifth was where the Eagles would remain come the end of the season. A 2-1 win at Gillingham was followed by two more draws at home, 0-0 with Aldershot and Chesterfield, before a 2-1 defeat at Chester. Before this last match, Hereford were crowned as champions, and Millwall and Cardiff joined them in the Second Division, as Brighton and Palace both missed out.

The season that had started so well, with Palace roaring ahead at the top of the table and going on a giant-killing spree to the FA Cup semi-finals, had finished with a crushing low. Fifth place was simply not good enough for a team that had shown what it could achieve with those cup wins. It was not good enough for Malcolm Allison either, and he resigned in May 1976.

Chapter 6

Venables Has the Eagles Ascending

THE PROJECT had stalled and it needed a lifeline. Two years in the bottom half of the Second Division and time spent in the Third Division are not a good way to reboot a club. The 1976/77 season was going to be a year of change. The weight of not getting to Wembley during the FA Cup run, his extracurricular activities and Palace failing to gain promotion had led to Malcolm Allison resigning. According to David Tossell's book *Big Mal: The High Life and Hard Times of Malcolm Allison, Football Legend*, the board also wanted Allison to accept a transfer fee of £300,000 for Peter Taylor to Leeds. The club badly needed the money, but Big Mal had stood firm. However, once Terry Venables took over as manager, Peter Taylor was transferred to Tottenham Hotspur for £200,000. The money was a good thing for the club, but the team had lost a major talent.

Quite simply, anything less than promotion would be a bad season. Not that all Allison did was bad, or just about himself. He wanted to build a club to last after he was gone. He wanted a club to turn out the players who could either be good enough to stay in the first team or be sold for large transfer fees. Coming through at West Ham as he did, the process of elevating players from juniors/youths was nothing new to him. The FA Youth Cup had come into existence in the 1952/53 season and was the most desirable trophy for all under-18 teams. In order for Palace to ascend up the pyramid, they needed a youth set-up to fill out the ranks. They had never been a wealthy club, and any money they made through transfers would go right back into the squad.

Academies weren't around at the time, so the young players had to get time in the reserves, out on loan or in the FA Youth Cup. The Youth Cup, like the FA Cup, gave non-league clubs an opportunity to pit their players against league teams in the qualifying stages of the tournament. There are a handful of clubs who are synonymous with the tournament, particularly Manchester United, West Ham and Crystal Palace. The Busby Babes became a legendary team, winning the first edition of the tournament.

Crystal Palace won the Youth Cup in 1977 and 1978, beating Everton and Aston Villa. The team included Terry Fenwick, Vince Hilaire, Steve McKenzie and Peter Nicholas. One of the coaches helping Allison and Venables was Chelsea's legendary defender Ron

'Chopper' Harris's younger brother Allan, who was part of Chelsea's back-to-back Youth Cup wins in 1960 and 1961, a team that included Terry Venables. After the win against Everton in the FA Youth Cup in 1977, youth coach John Cartwright could call on the services of his players again for the 1977/78 campaign. Some were already gaining first-team experience in the Third Division under Terry Venables, such as Kenny Sansom, Ian Walsh and Vince Hilaire, which was all valuable for the upcoming season.

The 1978 Youth Cup run began with a single-goal victory over Fulham at Selhurst Park in December 1977. In February, Chelsea were beaten 3-0. Victory over Leeds saw Palace through to the fifth round, where Port Vale were sent packing after a 3-0 win. The two-legged semi-final saw Palace drawn against West Bromwich Albion, which went to four matches in 17 days before a winner emerged. The first leg at Selhurst Park ended 1-1, before the return at The Hawthorns finished 0-0. The third match took place three days later at The Hawthorns, ending in another draw, this time 2-2. Back to Selhurst Park, where Palace finally killed it off, winning 3-0.

The final was at the neutral ground of Highbury, where Palace faced face Aston Villa. A sizeable number of Palace fans found their way to the match where, just like the season before, the cup was won by a single goal. After the two cup wins, Venables began to use more of the youngsters in the first team in Palace's climb up from the third tier. In fact, six of the players who were in that famous win against Burnley that later took the team up to the First Division came through the youth-team ranks.

Under Venables, Palace had to kick on for promotion in 1976/77. Their season started with a 2-2 draw against Portsmouth at Selhurst Park in the League Cup, with Dave Kemp scoring both goals for the Eagles. Palace came through the replay three days later with a 1-0 victory, after Peter Taylor, still to move to Spurs, scored the winner. He then scored the only goal again as Palace got off to a winning start in the league, defeating York City 1-0 at Selhurst Park.

Fixtures were coming thick and fast as three days later Crystal Palace travelled to Grimsby for yet another 1-0 win, thanks to Kemp's goal. Then three days later it was 1-0 again, but this time Palace lost away to Tranmere. To close out August, on the final day of the month Palace entertained Fourth Division Watford in the League Cup but surprisingly went down 3-1 to exit the tournament.

September started where August left off, as Palace struggled to score goals. Again they managed only one at home to Chester, but unfortunately their opponents scored two. However, the single-goal hoodoo was finally broken at home to Bury when the Eagles triumphed 2-1, but they then made up for this by failing to score in a goalless draw at Peterborough. Although they weren't conceding many goals, the Eagles certainly needed to start finding the back of the net if they were to deliver their promotion hopes, which they did in the next match when defeating Mansfield 2-0. However, at the end of September, after playing seven matches, Palace were down in tenth place in the table, although only two points off early leaders Brighton.

The Seagulls were Palace's next opponents, sharing the points in a 1-1 draw at the Goldstone Ground. The remainder of October saw Palace draw at home to Oxford and lose at Preston before defeating Rotherham and Shrewsbury. The month ended with a disappointing goalless draw at struggling Walsall to see Palace in sixth place but not looking like promotion candidates at this stage.

November started with two more draws, away at Swindon and home to Reading, before a defeat at Sheffield Wednesday. Palace then faced Brighton away again, this time in the first round of the FA Cup, where the Eagles came away with a 2-2 draw to force a replay. This again ended level, 1-1 after extra time. Before the second replay, which was twice postponed due to bad weather, Palace yet again drew, this time at home to Chesterfield, as the Eagles dropped to ninth in the table, with Brighton still leading the way. In December the FA Cup tie was finally decided when Palace beat Brighton at the neutral Stamford Bridge 1-0 to progress to the second round, which they played just five days later, defeating non-league Enfield 4-0.

However, another home draw in the league, 1-1 with Northampton, saw Palace enter the busy Christmas period in eighth place, having now drawn eight of their

18 matches and only scoring 18 goals. However, they were only six points behind leaders Brighton and had a match in hand. The Christmas and New Year period can have a significant impact on a club's season, and Palace got off to a flyer with a 3-0 away win at Gillingham. New Year's Day saw another draw, 0-0 at Reading, but then another 3-0 victory just two days later, this time at home to Walsall, although there was no change in Palace's league position.

Next up was the third round of the FA Cup and a plum tie against the mighty Liverpool at Anfield. There would have been no complaints at the goalless draw this time as the Eagles came away with a commendable result to bring the Reds back to Selhurst Park. Three days later Palace put up another great display, at one stage leading 1-0 as they took Liverpool all the way, eventually losing 3-2 in front of over 42,000 spectators.

Now out of both cups and sitting six points off the top spot in the league, Palace needed to get their act together if they were to gain promotion. Grimsby Town were first up, at Selhurst Park, where Palace won 2-1. Seven days later at bottom club York City, Palace stumbled to a 2-1 defeat. February therefore needed to be a much better month if Palace were to contend for the promotion spots. It started well, with a 2-0 home win over Port Vale, then a 1-0 victory at home to Tranmere, before disappointment in defeat at Chester. However, wins at Bury and at home to Portsmouth, before the month ended with a goalless draw at home to Peterborough, at least saw the Eagles moving up the table. They now sat fifth, still only six points behind leaders Brighton and three behind the promotion spots.

After an improved month, inconsistent form in March looked to have scuppered any hopes of Second Division football next season. It started with a 1-0 defeat at Mansfield, who now sat second in the table, but that was followed by an excellent 3-1 win over table-topping Brighton. However, Palace's up-and-down form saw them easily beaten at Northampton, 3-0, before winning away at Oxford. Although Palace weren't losing ground in the promotion chase, neither were they gaining any on their rivals Brighton, Mansfield, Rotherham, Wrexham and Preston. It was one of those rivals, Preston, up next at Selhurst Park, where Palace came out on top, 1-0. March ended with Palace still in sixth, five points behind new leaders Mansfield but four points away from the promotion places.

Palace needed a good run-in to the end of the season. It started with a 1-1 draw at promotion rivals Rotherham at the same time as Brighton were beating Mansfield, and Preston and Wrexham were both losing. It was therefore a point gained for the Eagles over some of the other contenders. A 3-1 home win over Gillingham then saw Palace move up a place, ahead of Preston, closing the gap to the leaders to just three points, although having played one more match than Brighton, who looked to be hitting good form. Another Palace draw, at lowly Portsmouth, gave no signs that Palace would hit a good run of form themselves, though, as Bury now joined the battle at the top of the table.

Palace finally found their goalscoring form in mid-April with a resounding 5-0 victory over Swindon, before being brought back to earth by a 1-1 draw at Shrewsbury. One step forward, one back. However, more goals were to come – 4-0 at home to Sheffield Wednesday, which saw Palace move up to fourth place, although five points off third and six points off the top. And it was one step backwards again when Palace were thumped 4-1 away at Port Vale. Just four matches now remained to close the five-point gap to the promotion places held by Wrexham and Mansfield, as Brighton led the way, one point further ahead of the Eagles.

As rivals Wrexham and Brighton played out a goalless draw, Palace gained ground with a 2-0 win at Chesterfield on the last day of April. Mansfield and Brighton now looked to be fighting it out to be champions, but Palace's crucial 2-1 home victory over Wrexham now saw them only two points behind their opponents, albeit having played one more match. It was still Wrexham's to lose, and they again slipped up by drawing their next match as Palace moved to within a point after beating Lincoln 4-1. Three days later, Brighton lost their penultimate match, so Mansfield had a two-point lead at the top, with Wrexham, who had two matches still to play, a further two points behind, followed by Palace a point behind the Welsh team. It was all to play for in the final week of the season.

Former Manchester City manager Malcolm Allison arrives at Crystal Palace.

Crystal Palace manager Malcolm Allison holding up three fingers to the Chelsea fans at Stamford Bridge, forewarning them of the final score. Crystal Palace won the match 3-2.

Vince Hilaire in action during a League Division Two match against Brighton and Hove Albion at Selhurst Park on 7 October 1978.

Crystal Palace manager Terry Venables in good voice with his players at a training session.

Kenny Sansom, Crystal Palace. It was his transfer to Arsenal that destroyed the club

Crystal Palace goalkeeper John Burridge poses with a comedy mask by the 'Keep off the Pitch' sign during a photocall. As a greenkeeper he likes to keep his patch in good trim.

Palace's new signing Mike Elwiss leaps over goalkeeper John Burridge during a photocall. John Burridge is wearing a comedy mask.

Wolves' Kenny Hibbitt, coming between his team-mate Mel Eves (left) and Crystal Palace's Jim Cannon after the Palace goalkeeper Terry Gennoe was brought down.

Crystal Palace players left to right: Jim Cannon, Micky Droy and George Wood with manager Steve Coppell during a training session, 24 September 1985.

6 October 1979 – Football League Division One – Crystal Palace v Tottenham Hotspur – Gerry Francis takes the ball past Osvaldo Ardiles of Tottenham (right).

Crystal Palace's Gerry Francis (top) goes flying over Brighton and Hove Albion's Gerry Ryan.

Crystal Palace goalkeeper Paul Hammond (on floor) grabs the ball under pressure from Southampton's Mick Channon (second left) as team-mates Jim Cannon (centre), Phil Holder (left) and Ian Evans (6), and Southampton's Peter Osgood (right), look on.

FA Cup Final 1990 Crystal Palace 3, Manchester United 3 – Ian Wright scoring for Palace. Wright scored two goals in the match.

A mural depicting a quote from ex-Crystal Palace manager Steve Coppell about striker Ian Wright is seen prior to the Barclays Premier League match between Crystal Palace and Chelsea at Selhurst Park on 18 October 2014.

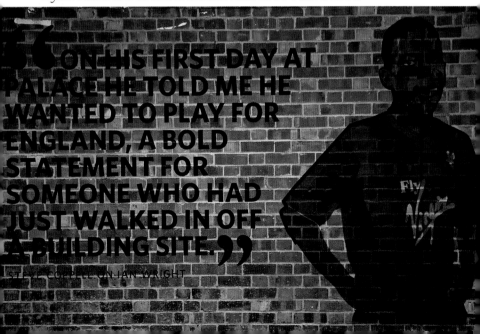

"ON HIS FIRST DAY AT PALACE HE TOLD ME HE WANTED TO PLAY FOR ENGLAND, A BOLD STATEMENT FOR SOMEONE WHO HAD JUST WALKED IN OFF A BUILDING SITE."

STEVE COPPELL ON IAN WRIGHT

The key match was up first. Wrexham vs Palace at the Racecourse. Palace saved one of their best performances for the final match, coming out on top 4-2. The two-goal margin could prove critical too. The Eagles had now overtaken Wrexham, who could still regain the third promotion place, but only with a win in their final match, as Palace now had the better goal difference by just one goal.

The final weekend of the league season saw Brighton draw, which meant Mansfield's victory gave them the championship. Even more important for Palace and their fans was that Mansfield's win was over Wrexham, so Palace could celebrate promotion to the Second Division.

Terry Venables had done what his predecessor couldn't achieve: win without the headlines. Big Mal was also unable to get the London team promoted. For such a young manager Venables was showing that he had the talent to push the club to a level it hadn't attained over the last few years. He had one advantage that Allison didn't, in that the youth players were starting to come through. The new gaffer was able to give debuts to the likes of Peter Nicholas, Billy Gilbert, Terry Fenwick, Ian Walsh and Vince Hilaire.

With Palace now one promotion away from the big time, the pressure was going to become more intense in 1977/78. It could hardly have started worse as the Eagles started the season in the League Cup first round by losing 2-1 to Brentford, two divisions below them, in the away leg. However, three days later they put this right by thrashing the Bees 5-1 at Selhurst Park. This form was then carried into the start of the league campaign when Palace convincingly beat Millwall at The Den, 3-0. And the goals kept flowing in the first home league match when three more were scored against Mansfield, who managed just one in reply. A great start, which saw Palace sitting top of the table.

Unfortunately, the great start didn't last long, as Hull went away from Selhurst Park with a 1-0 win, before Palace continued their League Cup campaign with a goalless home draw with Southampton. Suddenly the flow of goals had dried up. Two draws, a 1-1 draw at Burnley and 2-2 at home to Sunderland preceded the League Cup replay, in which Palace found themselves dumped out of the cup 2-1 at The Dell. However, they bounced back well with a 2-0 win at Sheffield United and a 2-1 home success against Bolton to end a reasonably successful month of September. Spurs unsurprisingly led the way in the league, followed by Brighton, Bolton and Palace.

October started with a derby at home to Fulham, but it was the away team who celebrated a 3-2 win in front of over 28,000 fans. Then a trip to the coast led to another defeat as Blackpool triumphed 3-1 and the Eagles began to slide down the league table. Palace then recovered their form to win at Stoke but their inconsistency showed as they then went down at home again, this time to Southampton. Palace's away form so far this season was outshining that of their home performances, and a share of the points with high-flying Brighton at the Goldstone Ground was another creditable outcome on the road, which is more than can be said of the same outcome at home to Charlton to see out October. Palace ended the month in eighth place but already seven points behind leaders Bolton.

A third successive 1-1 draw, this time at Oldham, saw the Eagles lose more ground to the leading teams at the beginning of November, which was made worse by a 2-1 home defeat to a strong Spurs team that was looking to bounce back to the First Division after their surprise relegation the previous season. Palace were now mid-table and hadn't won in five outings, which became six with a goalless draw at Orient. However, they finally gained maximum points with a 2-0 win at Selhurst Park against Cardiff to finish off a miserable month.

Unfortunately, December looked like being just as bad, as Blackburn, who had joined the promotion race, comfortably beat Palace 3-1 at Ewood Park. At this stage it looked improbable that Palace would join that race and get anywhere near successive promotions. Hopes were raised, though, by a 2-0 victory at home to Notts County and an impressive 2-2 draw at White Hart Lane against Spurs, for whom Glenn Hoddle scored twice, matched by Dave Swindlehurst for the Eagles. Boxing Day then saw another draw, a 3-3 feast at home to Luton Town, before a 3-0 defeat at Bristol Rovers the very next day. But at least the year ended on a high, as New Year's Eve saw a rare Palace victory, 3-1 at Mansfield. Despite the poor run, Palace went into 1978 in eighth, a reasonable position for their first season back in the Second Division, but some distance off the promotion places.

Just three days later, Palace won again, 1-0 at home to Millwall, before they entered the FA Cup in the third round, hopeful of progressing against Fourth Division Hartlepool. However, the Eagles suffered another surprise defeat by a team two divisions below them as Hartlepool ran out 2-1 victors, and this time there was no second leg for Palace to rescue themselves. Out of both cups early and not a great deal to play for in the league, and it was only January! Maybe this contributed to the disappointments that followed, a 1-0 defeat at struggling Hull City and a 1-1 home draw with second-bottom Burnley. However, Palace got the lift they clearly needed when they beat Sheffield United 1-0 at Selhurst Park, which was followed by a 1-1 draw at Fulham to see the end of another disappointing month.

March didn't start with a spring either, as Palace went down again at home, this time to Stoke City, but somehow the Eagles were still sitting in eighth place in a congested mid-table, as the top three of Spurs, Bolton and Southampton streaked ahead of them. One of those teams, Southampton, then inflicted another defeat on Palace, 2-0 at The Dell, the third time the Eagles had fallen to the Saints this season. Next up, the long trip to the North East to face Sunderland, where neither team could manage to score. The same result, this time at home to Brighton, probably summed up Palace's season.

Only six wins in 16 home matches, with just 22 goals scored, but only 18 conceded. But at least their home form was now better than their away form, which had seen just four successes in 16 away days, scoring just 17, although only conceding 19. Hardly scintillating stuff, although they still managed to attract 28,000 to the match against the Seagulls.

Another away defeat and no goals scored came with a 1-0 defeat at Charlton, as Palace now slipped to 11th, with several teams close behind, and the Eagles closer on points to the relegation places than the promotion race. At least any fears of slipping into the dogfight at the bottom were eased with a 1-0 home win over Bristol Rovers, one of those teams who had been close behind Palace, but March ended with another loss, this time at Luton.

April Fools' Day saw another goal drought at Selhurst Park as Palace and Oldham failed to find the net. A week later, as Arsenal and Ipswich reached the FA Cup Final, Palace played out yet another draw, but at least this time it was 2-2, at Cardiff. This was followed by the first win of the month for the Eagles, 1-0 at home to Luton, again struggling to score, but three valuable points. It didn't last, however, as league leaders Bolton put Palace back in their place by beating them 2-0 at Burnden Park. Bolton led the league by two points from Spurs and Southampton, with Brighton just two further points behind. The rest of the teams had been left trailing in their wake, Palace 13 points behind the Seagulls, but now safely 18 points clear of the relegation zone.

This buffer was just as well, as Palace went down again, this time at Notts County, 2-0, then dropped more home points by drawing 2-2 with Blackpool. Then came probably Palace's best performance so far, in the last fixture of the season, as they smashed five past fifth-placed Blackburn without reply. Where did that come from? This was on the same day that Bolton won the championship and Spurs and Southampton were promoted alongside them.

For Palace it was a mediocre season but at least it finished on a high, ending up ninth in the final table. There were some bright spots during the season. On 9 March 1978 goalkeeper John Burridge came in from Aston Villa, just 24 hours after Steve Perrin went to Plymouth. Burridge, always a character, was to become a fan favourite as the club reached the heights.

The following season of 1978/79 would be one of the most memorable seasons in Palace's history. Now Terry Venables had got the lads going, they just steamrolled the division.

In fact, they didn't lose a league match until the last weekend of October. The season commenced on 19 August with a 1-1 draw at Blackburn, but three days later saw Palace comfortably beating Luton 3-1 at Selhurst Park to kickstart their season. However, another draw 1-1 at home to West Ham didn't indicate that this season would be much of an improvement on the previous one, having already dropped four points in just three matches.

Palace then showed that they were capable of mixing it with First Division opposition as they defeated Bristol City 2-1 at Ashton Gate in the second round of the League Cup. Their next league opponents, Sheffield United, had shocked Liverpool by knocking them out of the League Cup on the same night, but were no match for Palace at Bramall Lane, the Eagles blunting the Blades 2-0. However, Palace's home form was still a concern as they failed to beat Sunderland, the scoreline being 1-1. The same scoreline at Stoke on the following weekend meant Palace remained behind that day's opponents, who led the league by one point from the Eagles, who were yet to set the season alight.

Midweek saw Palace once again perform well against First Division opponents in the League Cup, this time a 1-1 draw at Aston Villa to force a replay. A few days later it was the old foe of Brighton visiting Selhurst Park, where the Eagles came out on top, 3-1, thanks to a double from Hilaire. It was a win that took Palace to the top of the table as Stoke lost at Fulham. Back in the cup, a third match became necessary when it ended goalless against Villa after extra time, but that would have to wait until the following week. Meanwhile, Palace's improving form saw them win 3-2 at Preston, with Walsh grabbing a brace.

Unfortunately, they then went down heavily, 3-0 in the second replay of the League Cup tie at a neutral Highfield Road, Coventry, but they had shown that they could compete at that level.

Perhaps the number of matches they had played then affected Palace's form, as they struggled to a goalless draw at Wrexham in the league, but still retained top spot. At least now they would only have the league to focus on for a few months, but their first defeat was not far away, as they rounded off October by losing 1-0 to Fulham, who were third in the table, while Stoke moved back to the top. Then more disappointment was to follow as Palace went down 2-1 at Burnley to slip to third in the table, as West Ham moved above them.

Form and goals returned the following weekend as Blackburn were beaten 3-0 at Selhurst Park, Swindlehurst grabbing two goals. Up next was a crunch match away at West Ham, where it ended 1-1, a result that saw Palace go top as Stoke surprisingly lost 3-0 at bottom club Millwall. November looked like turning out to be a good month, as Palace beat Sheffield United again, this time 3-1 at home, but they then disappointingly drew 1-1 at struggling Cardiff. The end of the month still saw Palace on top, but only on goal difference from Stoke.

December started well, with a 1-0 home win over Newcastle, but again this was followed up by a draw, 0-0 at Notts County. Palace's home form was still looking good, as the Selhurst Park crowd saw them beat Leicester City 3-1. This meant seven victories from ten home matches, and 19 goals scored. Although only having lost once away, six draws from ten matches looked like a missed opportunity to be streaking away at the top of the table, which they led by only two points. This was re-emphasised two days before Christmas by a goalless draw at Cambridge United, although Stoke failed to take advantage when drawing by the same scoreline at Bristol Rovers. And it was mid-table Rovers who then provided a shock for Palace on Boxing Day by scoring the only goal at Selhurst Park, the only present for the Eagles being Stoke's failure to beat Charlton. The month didn't improve, as Palace were then held 1-1 at home by Orient. Another team in mid-table, and more points dropped.

The start of the new year traditionally sees the big guns entering the FA Cup in the third round, and Palace, despite struggling against mediocre teams in December, pulled off an impressive 1-1 draw at First Division Middlesbrough. It seemed the better the opposition, the better Palace performed, which at least augured well if they managed to achieve promotion come the end of the season. They proved this to be the case when they beat Middlesbrough 1-0, thanks to a rare goal by Kenny Sansom, in the FA Cup replay. Then they proved their inconsistency again by only drawing 0-0 at home to still-bottom Millwall the following weekend! Just to force home the point, Palace then beat First Division Bristol City in the fourth round of the FA Cup. Not only did they beat them but they trounced them 3-0 at Selhurst Park to really show their First Division credentials.

But first they had to get there, and their cup exploits had seen them slip to third in the table as the Seagulls flew to the top, with Stoke still in contention in second.

Palace, though, now had a match in hand, but would need to win it to move ahead of the others. In fact, one of their main opponents, Stoke, were the next visitors to Selhurst Park, but Palace failed to gain ground following a 1-1 draw. In a tough run of fixtures, Palace then faced Brighton away, again honours even, 0-0. All three teams were now on 33 points, Brighton having played one more match than Stoke and Palace.

Palace played out their third consecutive draw in a goalless affair at home to Preston, while Brighton and Stoke both won away from home, and West Ham and Sunderland closed the gap on the Eagles. Perhaps, then, Palace's defeat in the fifth round of the FA Cup wasn't such a bad thing, as it appeared that the famous trophy was proving to be a distraction from their title challenge. They went down 1-0 at home to First Division Wolves, so again no disgrace against top-tier opponents. Now to focus on the league, where West Ham had entered the promotion fray ahead of Palace, who were down to fourth.

Into March, Palace needed to put a good run of results together, and it started with a muted 1-0 win over Wrexham. Brighton won, but Stoke beat West Ham, so at least one of Palace's promotion rivals had lost ground. Two league wins in a row had been a rarity so far this season, and so it continued, with a goalless draw at Fulham, but the other promotion chasers failed to take advantage, all four teams taking one point. This helped Sunderland, who won to leapfrog both West Ham and

Palace into third. It was now a five-horse race, with just five points separating first and fifth.

Palace brought Sunderland's surge to a brief halt when they beat them 2-1 at Roker Park in front of nearly 35,000 fans. Another good result against the teams at the top of the table, this one a proverbial six-pointer that saw Palace move ahead of their opponents into third. And this time Palace managed to string two wins together as they next won at Luton 1-0. However, two did not become three, as a 1-1 draw at Charlton also saw Sunderland back in contention after they won at Stoke. At this stage the leadership was still in Palace's hands, as they had two matches in hand over Brighton, who led them by three points. But it would mean two wins for Palace.

In a full league programme on the last day of March, Palace won 2-0 at home to Cardiff. Meanwhile Brighton and West Ham only drew and Stoke lost. Sunderland were the only others of the top five who won, so Palace were now second, two points behind the Seagulls, with those two matches still in hand. But again Palace could not gain consecutive victories, drawing 0-0 at Oldham, an opportunity missed to go level on points with the leaders, although with an inferior goal difference. In fact, all the contenders were ruing a missed opportunity the following weekend as none managed to win. Palace lost at Newcastle, while the other four teams all drew, so at least Palace only lost one point.

Their trump card was the match in hand, but it was yet another missed opportunity, 1-1 at home to

Cambridge. Having had the chance to go top with a win, Palace remained third with six matches to go, a point behind Brighton, and level on points with Stoke. Sunderland had a match in hand and were only a point behind Palace, while the Hammers were still in the hunt, only five points off the leaders, with two matches in hand. It was all still to play for.

Brighton and Sunderland both won before the others played again. Palace slipped to fourth. All the teams were then in action on 14 April. Palace won at Bristol Rovers, but crucially Brighton lost. There were, though, victories for West Ham, Sunderland and Stoke. Still only five points separated the top five, and the Hammers now had three matches in hand over long-time leaders Brighton.

The following weekend, Brighton returned to form with a 3-0 win, while West Ham and Stoke both drew and Sunderland lost. Palace played the following day, and this time took advantage by beating Charlton 1-0 at Selhurst Park. This moved them up to third but they could go top by winning their match in hand. One opportunity taken, another lost, as Palace drew 1-1 at Leicester on the Friday night to remain third in the table. Three teams now had 51 points, but Palace's goal difference was inferior to the other two, so points would be crucial in the final three fixtures. In fact, wins for Sunderland and West Ham in their matches in hand could see them join the others on 51 points in what was turning out to be a fascinating battle for promotion to the top tier.

On the Saturday, with Palace having already played, Brighton and West Ham only drew, but Stoke and Sunderland recorded victories. Stoke had overtaken Brighton to lead the table, and Sunderland had leapfrogged Palace into third on goals scored. West Ham then played one of their spare matches in midweek and kept themselves in the hunt with a 3-1 victory over Burnley. The following night Sunderland showed they meant business with a 6-2 thumping of Sheffield United. From almost nowhere the Black Cats had now crept up to lead the table going into the final two matches for the top three, while Palace had three matches to play and West Ham still had four to fit in.

All contenders played on 28 April, and Palace stayed in the race with a 2-0 home win over Notts County. Of the others, Brighton were the only winners, as West Ham and Stoke both drew, and leaders Sunderland surprisingly lost at Roker Park to Cardiff. Their lead hadn't lasted long as they now slipped to third. Brighton were back on top, with Stoke second. Palace sat fourth but, yet again, just one win from hitting top spot.

Back then the league fixtures didn't all finish on the same day, so the next weekend was a full programme, and the teams with matches in hand would have the advantage of knowing what they needed to do. Saturday, 5 May saw Brighton and Stoke gain promotion by winning their respective matches, but the league title was still up for grabs, as Palace won at Orient, 1-0, the crucial goal coming from Swindlehurst. Sunderland also won, but West Ham lost, so the Seagulls currently sat top, Stoke second and Sunderland third, all having finished for the season. Palace had one match left but would need to win it to gain promotion; however, that win would also give them the title by one point. West Ham were now out of it, despite having two to play.

If you were paying attention earlier, you'll already know what happens next but, just in case, here's a recap. On 11 May 1978, in front of nearly 52,000 supporters, Walsh and Swindlehurst scored the two goals that took Crystal Palace into the First Division. Not only that, but the 2-0 victory over Burnley saw the Eagles crowned as Second Division champions. At the final whistle there was a pitch invasion in celebration.

Not only did Palace win the league but they pipped Brighton by a single point at the death. The local Brighton papers had already been talking about the title and the champagne celebrations before the season finished. Making this even better for Palace, this so-called celebration for Brighton would take place on an aeroplane during the Palace match. It makes you wonder when they heard the result of the Palace match.

Palace achieved a lot of club records in their promotion season but one they didn't want was that, by only scoring 51 goals, they were the first club in the Football League since the Second World War to win the Second Division with that few goals. On the positive side, they played a record 11 matches undefeated at the start of the season and they conceded the fewest number of goals, 24, in a season. They also drew the most matches, 19, which is why it took them so long to hit top spot.

* * *

Not all projects start off well. Malcolm Allison, while at Palace, had a bad run of form in his managerial career. The confident man took his job too seriously but had fun. Football is a sport built for nostalgia, and for Palace fans they remember the heroes and try to draw comparisons between then and now. Not everything in the past is great, nor was the end of the Palace golden era that bad. The Team of the 80s happened, and at least it's something Palace fans have to look back on.

Going to a match in those days wasn't a particularly pleasant occasion. You could get a heady aroma of body odour, tobacco, booze and dodgy food. Trying to push forwards in the crowd could be a bad idea, particularly if the balance of the mass was moving the other way. You could easily end up injured. This was particularly risky when a goal was scored, when the pens would be like something from Dante's *Inferno*. However, the terraces were a cheap way to get into the match if you could hold your own. Just like the rest of the ground, the turnstiles were rickety old things, easy to hop over. Or you could squeeze two of you through at the same time for the price of one.

This period in the top flight was dominated by Nottingham Forest and Liverpool, but Palace managed to make their mark. Their lack of silverware and fame made them an unknown quantity in the eyes of the media. It's similar to how Watford flew under the football radar. And, like Palace, the Hornets developed some of the great Black players of the generation, such as Luther Blissett and John Barnes. Terry Venables had turned down the Arsenal job to be involved with Palace, and he then allowed the youngsters to come through the system at Selhurst Park. This glut of great youth players was coming through because of the progressive spirit of the club. Venables kept the young players' feet on the ground, not allowing them to become too big for their boots.

In 1978/79 Palace won the Second Division while only losing four league matches, conceding just 24 goals in 42 fixtures, showing a ruthlessness in defence. However, scoring was a problem, with only 51 goals, and this problem was to follow Palace into the top flight. After a great start to 1979/80, the slide to a mid-table finish, which you've read about, was largely down to scoring just 41 league goals. Ironically, the Eagles found the back of the net 47 times the following season, but conceding 83 goals and failing to win once away from home (and only scraping three draws) saw the Team of the 80s heading in the wrong direction.

Chapter 7

Early 80s – Palace on the Slide

IN MY opinion, the start of the Team of the 80s falling apart was the Clive Allen/Kenny Sansom transfer saga. On paper, the deal made sense. Allen was a great goalscoring prospect, something Palace desperately needed, but Sansom was a good young left-back who would go on to have a glittering career for club and country. Also part of the deal, moving from Arsenal to Palace, was backup keeper Paul Barron, but it's clear that the Gunners got the better part of the transaction in the long run.

With the line-up changed, Palace's first two matches of 1980/81 could hardly have been tougher. They first travelled to Anfield on 16 August to play champions Liverpool, losing 3-0. Three days later they opened their home campaign against North London's Tottenham Hotspur, improving on the goalscoring front but losing 4-3. Palace's cause wasn't helped by the dismissal of Vince Hilaire, with the scoreline 3-2 in Spurs' favour. Palace definitely looked to have resolved their previous goalscoring problems with the signing of Clive Allen, though, as he fired a hat-trick against Middlesbrough in a 5-2 victory at Selhurst Park to gain Palace's first points of the season.

Palace then made it an 11 goal difference in three matches when they beat Bolton 3-0 away in the first leg of the second round of the League Cup. However, the good run of scoring came to an abrupt end at Molineux the following weekend in a 2-0 defeat to Wolves. They did, though, progress in the League Cup with a 2-1 home victory over Bolton, with Allen again on the scoresheet. He then scored once more, but could not prevent a 2-1 league defeat at Coventry, which left Palace second from bottom of the table, with only two points from five matches.

Things didn't get any better the following week as Palace went down by the same scoreline at home to Ipswich, which relegated them to bottom place due to Leeds drawing against Spurs. It was a start to the season that they would never recover from, and things went from bad to worse when they were thrashed 5-0 by Everton at Goodison Park the following weekend.

Palace had a tough draw in the League Cup third round against Spurs but gained a creditable goalless draw at White Hart Lane in the first leg, a far cry from the 4-3 thriller a few weeks previously. But in the league it was all doom and gloom after another home defeat, 1-0 to Aston Villa. Any hopes of a League Cup run were then destroyed, as Palace lost at home again, 3-1 in the second leg to Spurs, with only a Clive Allen penalty to show for their efforts.

Palace's home form was certainly a major cause for concern, not helped by losing 1-0 to West Brom the following weekend. Three home defeats in a row, and their away form wasn't helping the cause, as they next went down 1-0 at Sunderland. Still bottom of the table, with just two points from ten matches, although not yet cast adrift of the pack, as Manchester City were only two points better off, Norwich four points, and Brighton and Leicester five. All was not yet lost if a good run of form could be found.

That looked possible when Palace finally won again, at home to fellow strugglers Leicester, Hilaire and Allen providing the crucial goals that took them above Manchester City on goal difference. And the future looked more rosy when Palace took two more points at home to Southampton, with a 3-2 victory thanks to a Mike Flanagan hat-trick.

The short run of good form soon came to an end at Elland Road in a 1-0 defeat to Leeds, which, coupled with two recent wins for Manchester City, saw Palace propping up the rest once again. They did gain a point away, their first of the season, in a 1-1 draw at Norwich, before November started with an excellent 1-0 win at home to Manchester United in front of Palace's largest home gate of the season, over 31,000. This victory had the added bonus of seeing the Eagles overtake the Seagulls, as Brighton slumped to the bottom. However, this was achieved without Terry Venables, who had left the club under mysterious circumstances to take over at his old club QPR in the Second Division. Ernie Walley was caretaker boss for the win over United, not a bad start, but defeat at Birmingham, 1-0, extinguished any faint glimmer of hope of a renaissance for Palace, who then lost again to Spurs in a goal fest, this time 4-2 at White Hart Lane. It was back to bottom place.

Any point against Liverpool in those days was a good one, and Palace achieved that in a 2-2 home draw that showed what they were capable of on their day. However, at this stage some consistency was needed, which the Eagles lacked, going down 1-0 at Stoke the following weekend, then losing 3-2 at home to Manchester City at the end of November. The only consistency now was the run of poor form that saw December start with a 3-0 defeat at Nottingham Forest, and Palace starting to lose touch with safety from relegation, seven points adrift of Norwich in 19th place. By the time of the Forest match, Palace had called on Malcolm Allison to return to the club in what looked like a forlorn effort to perform a miracle in staving off relegation.

Whether it was the Big Mal impact or not, Norwich were on the end of one of Palace's best performances of the season, a 4-1 victory at Selhurst Park, with Allen scoring twice to help their survival cause. It didn't last long, though, as this was followed by a 4-2 defeat at Southampton, while the Canaries recorded a win to restore their seven-point lead over the Eagles. It seemed that Palace were playing better against the top clubs, as they next drew at home to Arsenal, 2-2, but then, frustratingly, follow this with a 3-2 defeat at fellow relegation candidates Brighton.

The FA Cup third round provided a brief respite from Palace's league woes. However, a tough draw saw them facing Manchester City, and their hopes of silverware were dashed after a heavy 4-0 defeat at Maine Road. With only league survival to focus on for the remainder of the season, a point was gained, or perhaps lost, in a 1-1 draw with Stoke City, followed by a goalless draw at home to Wolves, both matches Palace would have been looking to win. By the end of January 1981, Malcolm Allison had gone, to be replaced by Dario Gradi, who had been showing great promise at Wimbledon in the Third Division.

It didn't start well for the new man as January ended with a 2-0 defeat at Middlesbrough, which meant Palace had still only gained one point on the road at 14 attempts. This became 15 when they next went down at Portman Road to top-of-the-table Ipswich, 3-2, which could be seen as another decent performance against a leading club. But then came the inevitable poor performance, losing 3-0 at home to mid-table Coventry City. February's woes became worse with a 2-1 defeat at Aston Villa, leaving Palace five points adrift at the bottom, but still only six points from safety.

However, six points became eight following a 3-2 home defeat to Everton, then ten after losing 1-0 at West

Brom. This was followed by another disappointing home defeat, 1-0 to Sunderland, but at least the run of defeats was halted by a 1-1 draw at Leicester, who themselves faced potential relegation, sitting just one off the bottom. Palace, on the other hand, looked destined for the Second Division following a 1-0 home defeat to Leeds, and a defeat at Manchester United by the same scoreline. As April commenced, Palace were now 11 points adrift at the bottom of the table.

One of those brief glimmers again surfaced with a 3-1 home win over Birmingham, but it was too little, too late, and normal service was resumed with a humiliating 3-0 home defeat by Brighton, who were themselves still in the relegation zone. However, for Palace, this defeat by the Seagulls was enough to see them relegated with three fixtures remaining. A not unexpected defeat at high-flying Arsenal followed, 3-2, before yet another poor display at Selhurst Park, losing 3-1 to Nottingham Forest. Palace therefore had one more away match to play to try to achieve their first success on the road in the league all season. They failed, although they did take a point at Manchester City, on the day that Aston Villa were crowned as unexpected but deserved champions of the First Division. The Eagles finished a full 13 points adrift of their nearest rivals, Leicester, who, along with Norwich, joined Palace in the second tier for 1981/82.

* * *

Another key reason why the Team of the 80s fell apart was Terry Venables leaving for QPR early in the season, even though Palace were bottom of the table at the time of his departure. However, rumours abounded that Palace were looking to bring in a new manager behind Venables's back. This was allegedly Blackburn's player-manager Howard Kendall, who instead went to Everton and led them to compete closely with Liverpool during the mid-1980s.

One of the problems the Palace board had was whether to sack Venables, given Palace's poor start to the season, or to back him to see the Team of the 80s project out. They had to judge whether it was simply a bad run of form or the beginning of a downward spiral. Keeping the supporters happy is never easy, and a real struggle for the board of directors. Raymond Bloye, Palace's chairman, was said to be pushing to remove Venables.

The real story of why Venables left is still unknown, but by the end of October 1980 he was on his way to QPR, where he had played just six years previously. He led QPR to the FA Cup Final in 1982, where they lost in a replay to Spurs, another of his old clubs. They then won the Second Division championship in 1982/83, and in their first season back in the top flight finished fifth in the table, qualifying for the UEFA Cup. All this while Palace watched on from the lower reaches of the Second Division. It makes you wonder …

When Venables left Selhurst Park, Palace's caretaker manager until December was first-team coach Ernie

Walley. Like his predecessor, Walley had played for Spurs and Palace, signing on at Selhurst Park in 1959. Although he started well in his caretaker role by beating Manchester United and his tenure included a draw with Liverpool, it was only ever intended to be a temporary arrangement. It was thought that Malcolm Allison was the best man to get Palace out of the hole they found themselves in, but it was too much even for Big Mal. He had certainly been busy since leaving Palace four years previously, coaching at Galatasaray in Turkey, then Plymouth Argyle and Manchester City.

Big Mal's return to Palace lasted just a couple of months and failed to ignite the team, as you've read, but it was an impossible situation by the time he took over, as it was for Gradi. He was appointed by new chairman Ron Noades, who had only recently departed Wimbledon himself. As for Allison, he went on to have a well-travelled career, first at Yeovil, Sporting CP in Portugal, Middlesbrough, and Willington in County Durham in the Northern League. This was over just three years, before he spent a couple of years in Kuwait, then returning to Portugal to coach Vitória du Setúbal and SC Farense. He returned to the UK in 1989 for a brief spell at Fisher Athletic before finishing his management career at Bristol Rovers. Certainly a mixed bag.

Not only were Palace shedding managers but players were leaving too. Allison sold John Burridge, Terry Fenwick and Mike Flanagan to old boss Venables at QPR. At the end of the relegation season, more key players went through the exit door, including Gerry Francis, another recruit by QPR. Meanwhile, Peter Nicholas joined his former team-mate Kenny Sansom in North London at Arsenal, and Dave Swindlehurst left for Derby County.

Not only were things grim at Selhurst Park in 1981, but in the UK the basic fabric of society and community were unravelling. Post-war austerity was long gone, and now unemployment and disenfranchisement were on the rise. The tough-love policies of the Margaret Thatcher Tory government were really hitting hard. There was a nationwide recession that affected almost every club at the time, as it made it hard for people on the dole to afford to attend matches. And the nature of the defensive football didn't exactly encourage the supporters to part with their money. The FA therefore introduced three points for a win rather than two from 1981/82 to try to encourage teams to go for the win and play more attacking football.

Furthermore, it was in the summer of 1980 that chairman Ron Noades decided to demolish the old Whitehorse stand. It was therefore closed for two years, so a smaller capacity meant less money coming in through the turnstiles at Selhurst Park. Palace spent a lot of money on a new stand, creating more debt for the club, which also contributed to the shedding of many players.

* * *

The decline of the Team of the 80s had commenced but now Palace were looking to bounce straight back up from the Second Division. Going into the new season, Clive Allen had been sold to QPR, with Stephen Wicks coming the other way. Stephen Hughes also came in, from Gillingham, but these weren't players of the quality that Palace had in 1980/81. It wasn't going to be easy for Dario Gradi to continue the good work started by Terry Venables.

At least the Eagles got off to a flyer in 1981/82, beating Cambridge United 2-1 at Selhurst Park, thanks to a brace of penalties by Paul Hinshelwood. However, they were brought down to earth by Norwich, losing 1-0 at Carrow Road against one of the other teams relegated from the top tier the previous season. The same scoreline at Hillsborough gave Sheffield Wednesday the three points, as it looked as if Palace's woeful away form from the previous season was going to continue. However, home form looked solid, as two Walsh goals provided a 2-0 win over Charlton Athletic.

The following weekend saw some familiar faces in the line-up as QPR hosted Palace at Loftus Road. And it was Venables's new team that came out on top, Palace succumbing to a third successive 1-0 away defeat. It was 1-0 again, but this time at Selhurst Park and in Palace's favour, as Vince Hilaire scored the only goal against Orient. So far, a 100 per cent success rate at home, but matched by the same level of failure on the road left Palace in tenth place. The pattern was then spoiled, and not in a positive way, as Palace went down 1-0 at home to Shrewsbury to finish off September.

October brought Palace's first away point as they drew 1-1 at Leicester, for whom a certain Gary Lineker scored. There was then the embarrassment of a 1-0 defeat at Third Division Doncaster in the first leg of the League Cup second round, as things started to look tough for Gradi. However, a 3-1 home win against Rotherham, followed by a rare away success, the first in over a season in the league, 1-0 at Wrexham, improved the mood at Selhurst Park. Palace had moved up to seventh, so looked as if they could make a challenge for promotion as the season progressed.

The feel-good factor didn't last long, though, as Derby County came away from Selhurst Park with a 1-0 victory, Palace old boy Swindlehurst scoring the winner to rub salt into the wound. However, Palace managed to avoid the giant-killing act of Doncaster in the League Cup by triumphing 2-0 at Selhurst Park, to take a 2-1 aggregate victory and advance to the third round. Then came that familiar feeling, a 1-0 defeat away, this time at top-of-the-table Luton Town. Palace had suddenly slumped down to 14th place and were already looking to be off the pace.

November saw manager Gradi and Palace part ways, with ex-player Steve Kember promoted from his role as a youth coach to the managerial hot seat, where he would stay for the rest of the season. However, it was to be a month of mixed fortunes for the Eagles. It started with a home defeat, 2-1 to Blackburn, but in the League Cup Palace got the better of First Division Sunderland,

1-0 at Roker Park, to record a giant-killing of their own and show what they were capable of. They then gained a point in a goalless draw at Oldham, before beating Norwich 2-1 and Bolton 1-0 at home.

However, after a promising ending to November, December started with defeat, 2-0 at Barnsley, before Palace faced First Division opposition in the League Cup fourth round. There was to be no further giant-killing, though, as Palace succumbed 3-1 at home to West Brom. Next up, there was cup success, however, as Palace entered the FA Cup in the third round. This time it was their job to avoid a massive upset as they faced non-league Enfield away. It was a close-run thing, the Eagles triumphing 3-2 thanks to two Hilaire goals.

After six weeks without league action due to cup ties, Palace must have been hoping that 1982 would bring some better form, but the home fans left disappointed after a 2-1 defeat to Sheffield Wednesday. This left Palace down in 15th place, with a few matches in hand on all the teams above them, but with no hope of entering the promotion race this season. Then it was FA Cup action again next, Palace progressing to the fifth round by defeating Bolton Wanderers 1-0 at Selhurst Park, so at least the season was bringing some cheer for the loyal fans. There was little to celebrate in the next league fixture, though, a goalless draw at Cambridge United, which left Palace only three points clear of the relegation dogfight. And it was another goalless draw to end the month, this time at home to QPR, Venables's team ending the day nine places above Palace.

Palace's winless run continued into February when they went down 2-1 at Charlton to slip to 18th in the table, now only one point above third-from-bottom Cardiff City. Relegation was a concern, but it was now the FA Cup fifth round and a real opportunity to progress, as the Eagles had been drawn against fellow Second Division Orient at Selhurst Park. However, neither team could manage a goal, so a replay was needed, which meant fixtures were beginning to pile up for Palace. At Brisbane Road three days later Palace took the honours and a place in the next round of the FA Cup with a 1-0 victory, but they knew they desperately needed a similar result in their next league fixture against the same opposition to address their descent. They didn't get it, as again neither team could break deadlock as it ended 0-0.

February then ended with yet another defeat for Palace, 2-0 at Rotherham. Fortunately fellow strugglers Cardiff also lost, so Palace avoided the bottom three, and it was the team from the Welsh capital up next in the league. Before that, though, came the FA Cup quarter-finals, where five of the eight teams were from the Second Division. Palace faced none other than QPR, at Loftus Road, and it was Venables who was celebrating as his team scored the only goal, to maintain their hopes of a Wembley visit.

Palace now had only the league to occupy them, and they finally took three points, beating rivals Cardiff

1-0 to lift the gloom at Selhurst Park. However, on the road Palace were still struggling, well beaten 4-1 at the Baseball Ground by Derby County. They had won just once on their travels in the league all season, although that was still once more than the previous season! Then, surprisingly, they got that all-important away win by defeating mid-table Chelsea 2-1 at Stamford Bridge, a victory that saw Palace move up to 16th and put some much-needed space between them and the bottom three.

With matches in hand, Palace should now be safe from relegation, but next up they faced top-of-the-table Luton at Selhurst Park, coming away with a creditable 3-3 draw. However, the decent run soon faltered when Gary Lineker helped Leicester to a 2-0 win at Selhurst Park, then Palace went down again, 1-0 at Blackburn. March ended with a decent 0-0 result at Newcastle, but Palace were now being dragged back into the relegation fight, only three points above Wrexham and having played most of their matches in hand.

On the day that QPR beat First Division West Brom to reach the FA Cup Final, where they would face Venables's old team Spurs, conversely Palace were busy scrapping for Second Division survival. And it was a disastrous 3-0 home defeat to bottom club Grimsby that left them only two points clear of the bottom three, as Wrexham gained a point at home to Derby. The team from North Wales then recorded a valuable 4-2 win over Newcastle to leave the Eagles just one point ahead of

Bolton, three clear of Orient and only five in front of Grimsby at the very bottom.

Palace faced a tough match next, away at second-placed Watford, but again they performed better against one of the top teams, coming away from Vicarage Road with a 1-1 draw, John Barnes scoring for the Hornets. Then, having recently gained a much-needed away win at Chelsea, Palace went down at home to the same opposition, 1-0, in front of their largest home gate of the season of over 17,000, mostly disappointed, fans. With other results not going their way, Palace now found themselves in the bottom three and it looked as if successive relegations were on the cards.

These fears were eased slightly by a resounding 4-0 home win over Oldham Athletic on 17 April, but then more so three days later after a rare away win, 1-0 over Grimsby, to avenge their recent home defeat by the Mariners. The two wins shot Palace up to 14th in a closely fought league table, five points clear of the bottom three, although still not safe, given their inconsistent form. A further point was gained in a 0-0 draw at Bolton but, worryingly, other clubs below Palace gained ground with better results. Even more worrying was the 3-0 defeat by Watford at Selhurst Park that left Palace just three points clear of the relegation zone once again.

Worse was to come with another home defeat, this time 2-1 to Barnsley, which reduced the gap to the bottom three to just two points. With just four matches to play, Palace needed to find points to avoid being dragged down to the third tier. However, May brought a third straight defeat, 1-0 at Shrewsbury, as Palace slipped to 18th, just a point above Wrexham in 20th and Cardiff in 21st, while Orient looked doomed, a further six points adrift at the bottom.

In a six-pointer against Cardiff the following weekend, Palace fans finally had something to smile about as the Eagles came away from Ninian Park with a 1-0 victory. Not only had they beaten one Welsh rival, but the other, Wrexham, had also lost, so two points from their last two fixtures should be enough for Palace to stave off relegation, given their superior goal difference. And it was Wrexham up next, at Selhurst Park, where Palace achieved safety with a 2-1 win, on the day that Luton Town became Second Division champions, something Palace fans could only dream of.

The final fixture of the season for Palace saw them go down at home to Newcastle, 2-1, but the result was academic. However, it rounded off a very disappointing season in typical style, a season that saw Palace start with hope of getting back into the top tier but ended with them down in 15th place. It wasn't good enough to save Steve Kember's job, so Palace were once again on the lookout for a new manager for 1982/83.

Ron Noades did his popularity at Palace no good when he hired Alan Mullery from Brighton. It was so poorly received that a group of supporters protested. Mullery and Terry Venables had been team-mates at Spurs in the 1960s but had become rivals as they vied for the captaincy role. This rivalry continued as they became coaches in the 70s, with their teams, Brighton and Palace, battling for promotion from the Third Division. It's said that Palace fans were also incensed that Brighton's nickname of the Seagulls was only brought about as a counter-chant to 'Eagles' at a match between the two clubs. Whatever the reason for the animosity, Mullery wasn't a popular choice to take over the reins at Selhurst Park.

Chapter 8

1982 to 1984 – Clinging On

AFTER A season of struggle in the Second Division, Alan Mullery would need to work some magic to get his new charges going well. Mullery had taken Brighton up to the top tier and managed to remain there, finishing a decent 13th the previous season, so he arrived at Selhurst Park with a good pedigree.

Such was Palace's fall from grace that their first fixture of 1982/83 was in the FL Trophy, in the group stages, where they earned a 2-2 at Third Division Brentford. Their next match in the tournament saw them face Fourth Division Wimbledon at Selhurst Park, winning 1-0, but at home in their next match they came unstuck against Third Division Millwall, 3-0. It was hardly an inspiring start to the campaign and didn't bode well for a promotion bid in the league once it got under way.

The league season started at the end of August with a 1-1 draw at home to Barnsley in front of fewer than 8,000 fans, the third-lowest crowd of the day in the Second

Division. Palace also had to enter the League Cup in the first round, defeating Third Division Portsmouth 2-0 at home in the first leg. However, back in the league it was another draw, 2-2 away at Rotherham, in front of even fewer fans, before Palace achieved their first league win of the season, 2-1 at home to Shrewsbury. This was quickly followed by their second success, again at home, 2-0 against Blackburn, to leave Palace unbeaten after their first four league matches, sitting in sixth place in the table. A promising start for new man Mullery.

Progress to the second round of the League Cup was achieved with a 1-1 draw at Portsmouth before a return to league action, but it was a dismal showing as Palace went down 4-1 at Carlisle. The Eagles looked to be repeating their previous two seasons' poor away form but at least their home form looked good, as they confidently defeated Middlesbrough 3-0. However, they were still looking for that first away victory of the season after coming away from Loftus Road with a point against QPR in a goalless affair, then losing 1-0 at Bolton the following weekend.

Palace did at least manage an away win in the League Cup second round, although it was at the expense of Fourth Division opposition, beating Peterborough 2-0 in the first leg to all but secure their place in the next round. But it was business as usual back in the league with a 2-0 defeat at Burnley, as the Eagles slipped to mid-table, already losing pace with the top-three battle in which old rivals QPR were involved.

Thankfully, Palace's good home form continued, defeating Oldham 1-0, but the crowds were getting smaller, fewer than 7,000 turning out to watch. Newcastle had no such problem, as 22,000 turned out to watch them at home to Palace next up, but it was the same old story as the Eagles went down 1-0, the goal scored by Chris Waddle. Progress to the third round of the League Cup was achieved with a 2-1 home win over Peterborough, hardly inspiring, but a win nonetheless. And just as uninspiring for the fans at Selhurst Park was a 1-1 draw with Fulham the following weekend, but at least they remained unbeaten at home thanks to Vince Hilaire's goal.

Into November, and that elusive first away win in the league still evaded Palace as they drew 0-0 at Chelsea. Then home form deserted them as they went down 2-1 to Sheffield Wednesday in the League Cup to exit the competition, before drawing 1-1 at home to Leeds United. However, 20 November finally saw Palace win away in the league when they scored the only goal to take all three points at Leicester City. But the month ended in the disappointment of a 4-3 defeat at home to Wolves, to end Palace's unbeaten home record.

Worse was to come at the start of December when Palace went down heavily at Grimsby, 4-1, the home team having started the season well after being bottom of the table for a large part of the previous campaign. But at least Palace's home form came back with a 2-0 revenge win over Sheffield Wednesday. Leading up to the busy

Christmas and New Year period, Palace secured a point in a 1-1 draw at Derby, but then disappointed with the same scoreline at home to Charlton. The very next day a Cannon own goal saw Palace go down 1-0 at struggling Cambridge United, to round off a disappointing Yuletide that saw the Eagles down in 15th place.

The new year started with Palace nearer the relegation places than promotion but at least New Year's Day gave some cheer, as they again defeated Leicester, this time 1-0 at home. Just two days later they were in action at Selhurst Park again, but this time only managed a 1-1 draw with Rotherham. The following weekend saw Palace enter the FA Cup in the third round, drawn at home to York City, two divisions below them. The Eagles struggled to a 2-1 win to progress. The following weekend saw more away-day blues as Palace went down 3-1 at Barnsley, their seventh away defeat in 12 matches, with only the one win.

Next came a dispiriting home defeat, 3-0 to QPR, for whom Palace old boy Clive Allen scored two. QPR were still flying high, second in the league and looking good for promotion, with Venables in charge. No such hopes for Palace, but their FA Cup dream continued when they scored the only goal to knock out top-tier Birmingham City in the fourth round. Beating First Division opponents seemed to be no problem, but it was then followed by a 1-1 draw at Shrewsbury, leaving the Eagles down in 17th place, just four points above the relegation places in what looked like being a repeat of last season's nerve-shredding end to the season.

Palace drew fellow Second Division Burnley in the fifth round of the FA Cup at Selhurst Park, but neither team could register a goal, so it would be back to Turf Moor for the replay. Before that, Palace finally secured a win, and a convincing one at that, 3-0 at home to Bolton. Then, on the day that cup opponents Burnley hit seven past Charlton, Palace couldn't score at Oldham, going down 2-0. Burnley were not as prolific in the FA Cup replay, but managed to score the single goal needed to deny Palace a quarter-final place.

As March commenced, Palace now needed to focus on league form, but at Selhurst Park went down 2-0 to Newcastle, with Waddle again on the scoresheet. Goals were increasingly looking hard to come by for Palace, who again failed to score in their next match, losing 1-0 at Fulham to slip back down to 17th in the table, now just two points above third-bottom Cambridge United and only six points off the bottom. Relegation fears weren't eased by a goalless draw at home to Chelsea, followed by a 2-1 defeat at Leeds, results that left Palace in 19th, ahead of third-bottom Rotherham only on goal difference, and bottom team Burnley by just three points.

Although disappointed by a goalless draw at home to Cambridge United at the start of April, it proved to be a valuable point for the Eagles as their relegation rivals all lost and Charlton slipped into the bottom four. However, the following week Palace went down to that very team, 2-1 away in a six-pointer. Far from being like the previous season, this one was turning out worse, as Palace were now second from bottom as Derby had beaten Newcastle. With Cambridge winning in midweek, they had moved up the table, and just one win for Palace would see them do the same in what was a tight battle involving the entire bottom half of the league table. Any one of 11 teams, with a bad run of form, could go down at the season's end.

Palace eased their fears the following weekend with a much-needed three points, defeating Carlisle 2-1. This saw them leap up to 17th, although still level on points with the relegation places. Goal difference could prove vital in this closely fought race to the Third Division. In midweek, Derby and Charlton drew to take a point each, dropping Palace to 18th, which became 19th the following Saturday as the Eagles went down 3-0 at Blackburn, not a good result, or good for the goal difference. A 2-0 home win against Grimsby clawed some of the goal difference back, but it was the points Palace really needed; however, they failed to get either at Wolves on the last day of April, going down 1-0.

On Monday, 2 May, QPR were crowned Second Division champions after beating Fulham 3-1. Wolves also gained promotion but were seven points behind the champions. At the other end of the table, with just four matches to go, Palace really needed a couple of wins, but next up were in-form Derby County, who had fought their way up from the relegation battle to 14th.

By the time the match came around, Palace were back in the bottom three, but a resounding, and unexpected, 4-1 win moved them up to 17th, although only a point above the relegation places and still in need of points from the remaining fixtures. Their cause wasn't helped by going down to third-bottom Middlesbrough 2-0 in midweek, a result that took Boro up to 14th and left Palace needing three points from two matches to ensure survival.

Palace's cause was helped as Bolton lost and were relegated the following weekend. Meanwhile, Burnley gained a point at promoted Leicester, and Rotherham did the same at Leeds, but Palace lost 2-1 at Sheffield Wednesday, so it was all down to the final match of the season, which would see a fight-out between Palace and Burnley at Selhurst Park. Palace needed a draw to survive, Burnley needed to win. The largest crowd of the season at Selhurst Park, over 22,000, turned out to watch the Eagles score the only goal to secure Second Division football for another season.

It had been a close-run thing, and the so-called Team of the 80s was now only hanging on to second-tier status by its fingertips. Apart from the last match of the season, the supporters were staying away, clearly not happy with what they were seeing from Mullery's team and not adding to his popularity.

However, he was still there at the start of 1983/84, perhaps surprisingly, as nearly 14,000 watched Palace get off to a losing start at Selhurst Park, going down

2-0 to Manchester City, who had been relegated the previous season. Palace then comfortably beat Fourth Division Peterborough 3-0 at home in the League Cup first round, first leg, with Hilaire scoring twice, before gaining their first league point of the season in a 1-1 draw at Shrewsbury.

September started with a familiar away defeat, 2-1 at Huddersfield, then a 1-1 draw at home to Fulham, as Palace still sought their first league victory of the season after four attempts. Then came the embarrassment of going down 3-0 to Peterborough in the League Cup to level the aggregate score at 3-3. There were no further goals in extra time, so a penalty shoot-out would decide who progressed to the second round. Unfortunately, Palace failed miserably from the spot, going down 4-2 in an ignominious exit that didn't bode well for the season ahead.

The Eagles failed to pick themselves up for the next match, a visit to Newcastle, losing 3-1, leaving them second from bottom in the table. It looked like a long and tough season ahead, with only two points gained from five matches. By the time of their next match, Palace were bottom of the pile, but then gained their first league success of the season by defeating Portsmouth 2-1, moving them up a couple of places. One win became two, and this one a rare away victory, defeating Middlesbrough 3-1 at Ayresome Park. Not only that but a hat-trick of wins saw another away from home, this time 3-1 at Cambridge United. Two away wins in a row for the first time in a long, long time, and six goals to show for it.

Four in a row? Of course not, as Palace then went down 1-0 at home to struggling Derby County, to prove that their inconsistency hadn't gone away. Normal away form returned in a 2-0 defeat at Grimsby, but more worrying now was Palace's home form, as they next went down 1-0 to Barnsley. Five home matches with just one win and a draw achieved, which, given Palace's away form over the previous three seasons, looked likely to leave them in another relegation fight this season.

However, improved away form was continued with a 1-1 draw at Leeds, meaning eight of Palace's 12 points had come on the road. They then bucked that current trend somewhat the following weekend by beating Oldham 2-1 at Selhurst Park, but still maintained some semblance of away form by drawing 1-1 at high-flying Chelsea. Then a reasonably successful November ended with another home win, 1-0 over Sheffield Wednesday, leaving Palace solidly in mid-table, for once closer to the promotion battle than the relegation fight.

Unfortunately that form didn't extend into December, as Palace went down 1-0 at Swansea, then 2-1 at home to Carlisle, and it was back to being closer to the bottom three. The month then got worse as the Eagles lost their third consecutive match, 2-1 at Blackburn. There was no Christmas cheer either, as they lost at home again, this time to arch-rivals Brighton, 2-0 on Boxing Day. The Seagulls had been relegated the season before, having been runners-up in the FA Cup. In fact, they had been just one last-minute clear-cut chance away from winning the trophy, only to miss and then go down heavily to Man United in the replay, 4-0. The following day saw yet another defeat for the Eagles, this time away at Charlton, 1-0. The last day of 1983 at least saw Palace gain a point, but it was a disappointing 1-1 draw at home to Shrewsbury, to round off a thoroughly miserable month.

The Eagles ended the year in 18th place, just four points clear of the bottom three, although it looked increasingly likely that there was only one relegation place to avoid, as Swansea and Cambridge in the bottom two were a further seven points adrift and would need a miracle to survive. However, Palace's first fixture of 1984 was in the third round of the FA Cup, and once again they showed that they performed much better against higher-class opposition as they knocked out First Division Leicester City with a 1-0 win at Selhurst Park.

Palace couldn't transfer this form to the league, though, as they next went down 3-1 at Manchester City to continue their winless run. However, this was finally brought to an end with an unlikely 3-1 home win over fourth-placed Newcastle before the FA Cup returned. Again Palace were drawn against First Division opponents, West Ham United, but at Selhurst Park it ended 1-1 in front of over 27,000 fans. Three days later Palace's cup dream was ended at Upton Park, comprehensively beaten 2-0.

Back in league action in February, Palace recorded successive victories over opponents from the North East when they scored the only goal, from the penalty spot, at Selhurst Park against Middlesbrough, a win that took them six points clear of danger. This was followed by a 1-1 draw at relegation rivals Fulham, and the same scoreline at Barnsley, useful away points. However, this was then wasted by losing 1-0 at home to Grimsby, to spoil what had been a decent month, with Palace back down to 19th and six points ahead of Derby, third from bottom.

March commenced with a goalless draw at home with Leeds, but Derby's victory over Cambridge United closed the gap between them and Palace to just four points. Palace then lost 3-2 at Oldham, while Derby played in the FA Cup sixth round. Palace again drew 0-0 at home, this time against Huddersfield, but it was a point gained, as Derby went down at home to Brighton. Then a further three points were gained when Palace won 1-0 at Portsmouth. Having now both played 32 matches, the Eagles were seven points clear of the Rams with ten fixtures of the league season remaining. It may still be another nail-biter.

April Fools' Day brought a 1-1 draw for Palace at home to Cambridge, but Derby had been hammered 5-1 the previous day, so at least it was another point gained for the Eagles. However, next up was a six-pointer against Derby at the Baseball Ground. A win for Palace would surely secure Second Division football for another season, but Andy Garner had different ideas, as his hat-trick sealed a vital 3-0 win for the Rams to help their chances of survival, on a day that Oldham Athletic joined the relegation fight.

Derby lost in midweek but then picked up a point at the weekend, while Palace lost 1-0 at home to Chelsea, and Oldham also lost. Cambridge were relegated, so there were only two relegation places for Palace to avoid, and Swansea were all but down. The gap to Derby was now four points, but three days later increased to seven when Palace travelled to South Wales and came away with a 2-0 win over Cardiff City.

Easter weekend turned out to be a mixed one for all three relegation rivals. It started badly for Palace, losing 3-1 at Brighton, while Derby won, and Oldham had picked up a point in a Friday evening match. The topsy-turvy form of the clubs was evident two days later when Palace won 2-0 at home to Charlton, but Derby lost at Cardiff, so the gap was back up to seven. Oldham then lost the following day. Overall, it could be seen as a decent weekend for Palace as they had now also moved above Middlesbrough to 17th place, and they had maintained the seven-point gap, with only four matches remaining of the season. Meanwhile, Swansea had been relegated, so there was only one relegation place left.

By the time Palace played again, Oldham had lost at Leeds, but Middlesbrough had beaten Sheffield Wednesday, then lost at struggling Swansea. On 28 April Palace lost 1-0 at Sheffield Wednesday, which saw

141

the latter promoted to the First Division. Meanwhile, Derby kept up their hopes of survival with a 1-0 win over Manchester City, and Oldham did likewise by beating Portsmouth 3-2. With just three matches remaining, the dogfight at the bottom was still potentially between six teams, as just six points separated 15th and 20th in the table, but Palace had what must surely be the easiest match next as they faced relegated Swansea at Selhurst Park.

On 5 May, Palace finally secured their Second Division status, beating Swansea 2-0. Although Oldham also won, Derby's defeat at Newcastle meant that Palace were safe for another season, with two matches to spare this time. Derby were relegated the following weekend without playing, as Oldham won again. Palace gained a further point with a 2-2 draw at Carlisle, but their season ended in a 2-0 home defeat to Blackburn, consigning them to 18th place.

Palace's relegation fights didn't please the board, so Mullery departed, ironically to lead QPR, who Terry Venables had managed to an excellent fifth-placed finish in the First Division and qualification for the UEFA Cup. Venables was soon to become known as 'El Tel' as he departed to coach Barcelona, where he also had great success, including La Liga success and reaching the European Cup Final for the first time in 25 years.

Chapter 9

Mid-80s – Times
Are A-Changin'

IN MAY 1984 Dave Bassett, having just achieved consecutive promotions at Wimbledon to take them into the Second Division, accepted the manager's role at Crystal Palace. He was seen as an up-and-coming manager who was attracting the attention of other clubs due to his success at Wimbledon and the fact that his contract there was due to end in October 1984. However, within 72 hours Bassett had changed his mind and decided to stay loyal to the Dons.

Ron Noades's next big decision, and one that was to prove a shrewd one, was to appoint Steve Coppell. After eight years at Manchester United, and having gained 42 England caps, Coppell had retired as a player in October 1983, aged just 28, after failing to fully recover from a serious knee injury. The Liverpool-born winger had played a staggering 207 consecutive league matches for the Red Devils between 1977 and 1981, but in England's 1982 World Cup qualifier against Hungary a crude tackle by the Magyars' captain József Tóth shattered Coppell's knee. Although he returned for both club and country after an operation, he was never the same player and underwent further surgery. After two more seasons, a third operation was needed, but Coppell knew it was time to call it a day as a player.

At 28, Coppell was one of the youngest managers in the Football League and obviously had no experience in the role, so it was clearly a gamble by the Palace board to appoint an unknown quantity. Palace had now been struggling in the lower reaches of the second tier for three seasons, so he was under immediate pressure to show some improvement at the club in 1984/85.

Up first in the league were Blackburn at Selhurst Park on 25 August. It ended in a 1-1 draw, after Palace had taken the lead. Next it was the first round of the League Cup, where Palace looked to have a good draw against Northampton Town of Division Four. However, the first leg at Selhurst was anything but easy, Palace scraping home 1-0. And it was certainly not easy-going the following weekend when they were easily beaten 4-1 at Shrewsbury. Not a great start for the new man in charge, and yet another slow start to the season for the Eagles. They did, though, manage to progress in the League Cup with a goalless draw at Northampton.

The poor league form continued at Selhurst Park, going down 2-0 to Birmingham, to leave Palace with a solitary point from the opening three matches – coincidentally, the same as Wimbledon, who were also struggling. Next up were arch-rivals Brighton, and it was the Seagulls who went home happy after their 1-0 win at the Goldstone Ground, to leave Palace bottom of the table after four successive league defeats. On the day that QPR made their bow in the UEFA Cup in Iceland, Palace finally got up and running by defeating Sheffield United 2-1 at Bramall Lane, and better was to follow a few days later at Selhurst Park, Palace triumphing over another Yorkshire club, Leeds United, 3-1. Back-to-back wins took Palace up to 17th.

They had another chance to show their pedigree against top-tier opposition when facing Sunderland in the League Cup second round, but went down 2-1 in the first leg at Roker Park. Before the second leg, Palace's short winning run came to an end with defeat at Manchester City, 2-1, followed by a 1-0 home defeat to Barnsley. At home to Sunderland, neither team could break the deadlock, and the goalless draw meant Palace were out of the League Cup.

A fourth successive defeat, 1-0 at Carlisle, did little to lift the spirits for Palace, who slipped back down to 20th and looked set for another relegation battle. And three days after their old boy Kenny Sansom had scored for England in a 5-0 victory over Finland, Palace came unstuck again, losing 2-1 at Wolves, but at least a fifth successive league defeat was avoided by a 2-2 home draw against Fulham. If Coppell was feeling any pressure at this stage, and Dave Bassett was wondering whether he had made the right decision, Wimbledon beating Palace 3-2 at Plough Lane would have certainly left Bassett under no illusions that he had been correct, while Coppell must have been wondering whether management was for him. Wimbledon were comfortable in mid-table, while Palace languished in 20th spot.

The Eagles scraped another couple of points at home, 2-2 against Shrewsbury and 1-1 against Huddersfield, but these were matches they would expect to be winning. A third consecutive draw followed, 1-1 at Portsmouth, before the run came to an end with a victory at last, 3-0 at home to Oldham. But it was back to the draws again the following weekend, 1-1 at Middlesbrough, followed by another 1-1, at home to Cardiff, but at least Palace were on an unbeaten run of six matches. Six then became seven with a 3-1 victory at Grimsby, and things were finally looking hopeful for Palace, who had climbed back up to 17th and were looking difficult to beat, unlike the previous few seasons.

On Boxing Day, the Eagles extended their good run of form with a 2-1 home win over Charlton, but then finished off the year with an awful 5-0 defeat at Oxford United, who were vying for promotion. Notts County had been struggling near the bottom of the table all season, but Palace couldn't score against them on New Year's Day in a goalless encounter. After a promising run, Palace had come down to earth with a bump in the league, but now entered the FA Cup in the third round, away at Millwall, drawing 1-1. The replay saw the embarrassment of being giant-killed by their Third Division opponents, 2-1 at Selhurst Park.

February started badly, with another 2-1 home defeat, in the league by Manchester City, before Palace gained some semblance of revenge by beating Oxford 1-0 at Selhurst Park, a surprise result against the team that were now top of the table. However, this was followed by another defeat, 2-0 at Huddersfield that left Palace 18th in the table, only three points above the relegation zone. Sound familiar?

If Dave Bassett realised he had made a good decision to turn down Palace to remain at Wimbledon when his club beat Palace earlier in the season, his decision looked even more sensible when the Dons came to Selhurst Park and left with a resounding 5-0 scoreline in their favour, the second time the Eagles had shifted five goals so far this season. After a 2-2 draw at Fulham, Palace then began March with another draw, 0-0 at home to Wolves, as they began to struggle for a win again. However, at the fifth attempt it came, defeating Carlisle 2-1 at Selhurst Park, but it was followed up with a 3-1 loss at Barnsley. Then March ended with Palace looking over their shoulders after slumping to a 3-1 home defeat to Sheffield United. The Eagles were 18th in the table, four points above third-bottom Notts County, and only six points ahead of bottom club Cardiff. And next up were Brighton.

It ended honours even at Selhurst Park against the Seagulls, 1-1, then the same scoreline away at

Charlton, so at least Palace were picking up odd points here and there, but would it be enough? Three points was what they needed, and that's exactly what they got as they beat Notts County 1-0 to extend the gap over the bottom three. However, a heavy defeat, 4-1 to Leeds, followed, then another, 3-0 at Birmingham. It seemed like one step forward, then two back, but it was forward again in a 2-1 victory at home to Portsmouth in front of the largest gate of the season at Selhurst Park: 10,215.

That win eased the relegation fears considerably, if not Palace's league position, as they were now nine points clear of danger, and their main rivals only had four matches to play, so would need to produce results immediately. This became academic when Palace beat Blackburn 2-1 away, which virtually secured Second Division football for Steve Coppell's boys. It had been another struggle, but at least they had achieved this earlier than the previous couple of seasons.

There were still blips, though, as Palace next went down at Oldham 1-0 on the day that Oxford United were promoted to the top tier. Other results meant that the Eagles were still not safe, but just one win from their last three matches would be enough. May brought that all-important victory, 1-0 at home to close rivals Middlesbrough, so three wins in their last four matches had seen Palace move well clear of danger. They then ended their season with a 3-0 away win at Cardiff and a 2-0 home defeat to Grimsby, just to confirm their yo-yo tendencies. Oxford had won the league, while Palace had climbed to 15th after a good end-of-season run that must have given some confidence for the following campaign and hopefully a push for promotion.

Before 1985/86 kicked off, Palace signed a 21-year-old from non-league football, Ian Wright, who had been spotted playing for Greenwich. He was to go on to have a stellar career for Palace and Arsenal, and was a very shrewd signing, his fee allegedly being a set of weightlifting equipment! Palace started the new season in good style, with a 2-0 win at Shrewsbury in the league and 2-1 at Charlton in the League Cup first round, first leg. After a 1-0 win at home against Sunderland the following weekend, the promising start gave hope of a better season ahead after several in the doldrums. A draw away at Carlisle spoiled the 100 per cent record, before a surprise home defeat, 3-2 to Huddersfield, perhaps brought expectations back down to earth.

At the start of September, Palace progressed to the second round of the League Cup after drawing 1-1 at home to Charlton but then lost 3-1 to the same team away in the league. A goalless draw at home to Fulham meant that Palace had failed to win in their previous four league matches, and they had already slid down the table to 14th. What promised to be a better season was already looking like the same old story, and it didn't get any better when Palace went down 4-3 at Norwich in their next match. However, the poor run was ended at Selhurst Park with a 2-1 win against Millwall.

Next up for Palace was a League Cup tie against the mighty Manchester United, who currently led the First Division, having won all their matches so far. At Selhurst Park in the first leg, over 21,000 turned up to see a close encounter, with Palace losing to the only goal of the match, scored by Peter Barnes. A trip to Old Trafford beckoned but it would be an almighty task to overcome even that small deficit. September then ended with Palace drawing 0-0 at Stoke, while their League Cup opponents were making it ten wins from ten in the top tier.

October started in typical inconsistent fashion for the Eagles, going down 2-0 at home to Hull City, then winning 2-0 at Middlesbrough, before the second leg of the League Cup arrived. There was to be no shock giant-killing at Old Trafford, unfortunately, but Palace held their own again, only going down to a single goal, scored by Norman Whiteside. Back to league action, Palace made it consecutive victories by defeating Oldham 3-2 at home, Ian Wright scoring the all-important third goal for the Eagles.

On the night when Gary Lineker was scoring a hat-trick at Wembley as England thrashed Turkey 5-0 in front of over 50,000 fans, only just over 2,000 turned out to see Palace play in the Full Members Cup, where they lost 3-1 to Brighton. This tournament was created after the Heysel Stadium disaster, where fans rioted at the European Cup Final between Juventus and Liverpool. After a wall collapsed, 39 fans were killed and over 600 injured in the aftermath. Liverpool were held to blame for the incident, leading to a ban on all English clubs competing in Europe until 1990/91, and Liverpool for a further season.

Palace's recent good form in the league ended with a 1-0 defeat at runaway league leaders Portsmouth, which left the Eagles in ninth place, albeit an improvement on recent seasons. Meanwhile, the Full Members Cup brought another defeat, this one 2-1 at First Division West Brom, in what was clearly a meaningless competition, highlighted by the low turnout of fans. The league was what mattered most, and Wright scored again as Palace took all three points with a 2-0 win at home to Blackburn.

November started poorly, the Eagles going down 1-0 at Bradford City, before bouncing back at home to Grimsby with a 2-1 success, followed by an even better performance in beating Leeds 3-1 at Elland Road. Palace were now up to seventh, only four points behind second-placed Wimbledon. A third win on the bounce was then recorded with a 1-0 win at home to Barnsley, as Palace looked set for a serious promotion bid. A goalless draw at fellow promotion hopefuls Sheffield United ended the winning run but was still a decent result against good opposition, who were now sitting second, only a point behind Portsmouth, with Palace three points further adrift and well in contention.

December started where November left off, Palace looking like potential title contenders now after a 2-1 win at Hull. However, they looked far from promotion hopefuls when losing 1-0 at home to Shrewsbury, who had been struggling in the bottom three. The lead-up to the Christmas programme brought a 1-1 draw at Sunderland, before another home defeat, 3-1 on Boxing Day to Wimbledon, who were going well under Bassett and looking to move up to the top tier.

New Year's Day saw Palace facing old foes Brighton at the Goldstone, the home team coming out on top once again, 2-0, to dent Palace's promotion hopes. The Eagles had now fallen to ninth, while the Seagulls were up to fifth with their third consecutive win. For Palace it was no wins in four league outings. The FA Cup always brings some respite, but for Palace it was another home defeat and an early exit in the third round, losing 2-1 to First Division Luton.

With only promotion to play for, Palace got back to winning ways at home to Charlton, 2-1 victors, but then played out a goalless draw at Huddersfield in a match they would have expected to win. Less so their next match, against high-flying Norwich, but Palace had home advantage. However, it was the Canaries singing on the way home after a 2-1 win to maintain their top-of-the-table position. There was then further disappointment to start February, with a 1-1 draw at home to Carlisle, who were bottom of the table and well adrift of the rest, but Palace took three points for the first time in four matches by winning 2-1 at Blackburn to remain in touch with the promotion race.

These hopes were raised in early March by a 2-1 home win over Middlesbrough, but then hit by a 2-0 defeat at Oldham to leave the Eagles nine points adrift of Wimbledon in third and in need of a good run to get back into contention. Unfortunately, this didn't come, as Stoke took all three points from their visit to Selhurst Park, scoring the only goal of the match. Palace bounced back away at Fulham, winning 3-2 but their inconsistent form meant they looked unlikely to challenge for a top-three place in their final nine fixtures.

At least the run-in started well, a 1-0 home win over Brighton, which would dent the Seagulls' own promotion hopes. Then Ian Wright was on target to help gain a creditable 1-1 at Wimbledon, who were up in fourth place, five points ahead of Palace in eighth. On the day that Liverpool and Everton won their places in a Merseyside FA Cup Final, Palace were winning 2-1 at home to Bradford City to move within three points of third-placed Charlton. There were still hopes of a promotion bid, although Palace had played more matches than some of their rivals.

April continued in positive mood, as Palace next beat second-placed Portsmouth 2-1 at Selhurst Park to move within two points of the promotion places. One of those places was confirmed when Norwich achieved promotion the following weekend, but Palace came unstuck in style at Grimsby, going down 3-0, while fellow contenders Charlton and Wimbledon both won. But Palace kept their hopes alive with an impressive 3-0 home win over Leeds, as Wimbledon and Charlton both drew.

For Palace, 22 April was the day their promotion hopes died. As Charlton took three points at Fulham, Palace lost 3-2 at Millwall. The Eagles now only had two matches left and would need to win both, hoping that Charlton and Wimbledon slipped up. However, Charlton still had four left to play, and Wimbledon five, so they both had plenty of opportunities to gain the necessary points to leave Palace facing Second Division football next season.

Palace did their best, winning 4-2 at Barnsley with the help of a Wright double, but Wimbledon and Charlton both won, so the remaining two promotion places were between them and Portsmouth, while Palace could finish no lower than fifth. They drew their final match of the season, 1-1 at home to Sheffield United, while Wimbledon and Charlton achieved promotion behind champions Norwich.

Clearly, it had been a much-improved season for Palace under Steve Coppell, having stayed in the promotion race until the last couple of weeks rather than being part of the relegation fight at the other end of the table. The question was whether they could go one better in 1986/87, when a new play-off system was to come in that meant the 19th-placed club in the First Division would play off against the teams coming third, fourth and fifth in the Second Division to decide who would play in the top tier the following season. If Palace could maintain their improvement, they should be in with a good chance of at least being part of the play-offs.

Chapter 10

1986 to 1988 – So Close But ...

PALACE UNDER Steve Coppell now looked to be a force to be reckoned with in the Second Division, having improved dramatically the previous season under his leadership. After a few seasons spent staving off the drop to the third tier, perhaps now was the time for the Team of the 80s to salvage something from the decade.

The season of 1986/87 certainly started on a good note, winning 3-2 away at Barnsley, with Ian Wright opening his account for the season, then a home win against Stoke by the only goal of the match. The 100 per cent record was maintained at Bradford City with a 3-2 victory that must have had the fans anticipating a successful season ahead; however, the run came to an end at Derby in a 1-0 loss. Palace were soon back to winning ways at home to Huddersfield, 1-0, but then suffered their first home defeat of the season, going down 2-1 to Sheffield United. A mixed start to the league campaign still saw the Eagles sitting second in the table, though, as only table-topping Oldham had shown any consistent form.

Next up was the Full Members Cup, possibly an unwanted distraction, and the result was certainly unwelcome, as Palace went down 4-0 to Portsmouth. The fans also showed their lack of interest in this competition as only 2,515 turned out at Fratton Park, and the largest gate of the evening was under 7,000 at Roker Park.

Back in league action, Palace maintained their good away form when beating Blackburn 2-0, before they entered the League Cup in the second round, disappointingly drawing 0-0 at home to Third Division Bury in the first leg. It seemed that Palace's usually strong home form had deserted them, especially as they next went down at Selhurst Park 3-1 to Reading in the league. However, October saw the home fans happy as a 2-1 win over Millwall saw Palace top the league table for the first time in years. They then managed to sneak through in the League Cup with a 1-0 win at Bury, but came unstuck a few days later in the league, going down heavily at Leeds, 3-0. And it was another heavy defeat to follow, this time 4-1 at Birmingham, as Palace began to shift goals alarmingly, next going down 3-2 at home to Shrewsbury – ten goals conceded in their last three matches, and plummeting to ninth in the table.

In the League Cup, Palace had a tough draw against First Division Nottingham Forest, drawing 2-2 at home to force a replay, but their poor league form continued with a 3-1 defeat at Plymouth. The cup replay saw just a single goal, but unfortunately it was scored by Forest to end Palace's participation. What they really needed was a return to their early season league form, but they were conceding too many goals, three more shifted at home to Grimsby without reply. From top of the table, the Eagles had now lost five in a row, conceding 16 goals in the process, to sit mid-table.

In their next match, at Selhurst Park, Palace conceded three again, but at least this time they matched their opponents, Ipswich Town, to gain their first point in six matches, but next up were league leaders Oldham away. Palace at least restricted Oldham to a single goal, but unfortunately could not find one themselves at Boundary Park, a defeat that saw them slip down to 15th, a long way from the promotion race that they seemed certain to be part of at the start of the season.

What had been a terrible month for Palace at least finished brightly with their first win in eight league matches, and no goals conceded in a 2-0 home success against Sunderland. However, December started in what seemed to be familiar fashion, as the Eagles went down 2-0 at high-flying Portsmouth, but then came a quite startling turnaround as they finally hit some form, thrashing Hull City 5-1 at Selhurst Park. They followed this up with a more routine 2-1 win at bottom club Huddersfield, but it was two wins on the trot that must have given some hope of a revival and a push for the play-off places after Christmas 1986.

It started that way, Boxing Day bringing a welcome 2-0 win over old foe Brighton at Selhurst Park in front of over 10,000 fans, a victory that still left Palace down in tenth, but only three points off fourth-placed Ipswich. However, it was the Tractor Boys that Palace faced the next day, going down 3-0 at Portman Road to put a big dent in the Eagles' hopes.

New year, new Palace? They must have hoped so as they won 2-1 at West Brom on New Year's Day, then two days later beat Derby at home by a single goal. This improved league form was then interrupted by the third round of the FA Cup, in which Palace again faced Nottingham Forest, this time knocking their top-tier opponents out, 1-0 at Selhurst Park. Having shown their worth against First Division opponents, Palace then resorted to their usual inconsistency, going down 1-0 at home to Barnsley in the league, a team that was down in the lower reaches of the table. On the last day of January, Palace faced a tough tie in the FA Cup, Spurs at White Hart Lane, and the home team made no mistake, triumphing 4-0, Palace old boy Clive Allen scoring from the penalty spot.

February started as January ended, in defeat, Palace going down 3-1 at Stoke, before a poor 1-1 home draw with Bradford City, another team struggling at the wrong end of the table. The Eagles looked a long way from challenging for promotion when they went down to another defeat, 1-0 at Reading, leaving them 11th in the table, although only four points off the fifth place that would put them in the end-of-season play-offs. All hope was not lost, and the month ended with an encouraging 2-0 win at home to Blackburn to lift Palace three places in the table.

They had a two-week break before their next match, and the rest must have worked wonders, as they thrashed Birmingham 6-0 at Selhurst Park, Ian Wright hitting a brace. But it was back to reality next, as Palace went down 1-0 at Sheffield United. Still looking eagerly at the play-off places, Palace beat close rivals Leeds 1-0 at home to leapfrog them in the table, now up to sixth, but four points behind Plymouth in that all-important fifth spot. Meanwhile, Derby, Portsmouth and Oldham were way ahead of the chasing pack led by Ipswich.

A goalless draw at Shrewsbury continued Palace's frustrating form against teams at the bottom end of the table, but then an away win at mid-table Millwall brought them level on points with Plymouth, who had a match in hand. With eight matches remaining the Eagles were now in the fight for the play-off places and a shot at First Division football next season.

April increased those expectations as Palace beat Grimsby 1-0 away. Only goal difference separated Plymouth and Palace, so those earlier heavy defeats suffered by the Eagles could be costly come the end of the season. However, Plymouth slipped up in their next match, as Brighton did Palace a favour by holding the Pilgrims to a draw. Now having played the same number of matches, Plymouth led Palace by just one point, with seven matches to go, and the two due to face each other next up in what could prove to be a crucial encounter.

On the day that Clive Allen scored to help Spurs reach the FA Cup Final, Palace were focused on beating their main rivals for the play-off places. They had home advantage but could not make that pay as the match ended goalless, a result that favoured Plymouth more than the Eagles, for whom an opportunity had been lost. It was a result that also favoured Leeds, who were close behind and had matches in hand, the next of which they won to jump ahead of Palace in the table. Both Palace and Leeds tailed Plymouth by a point, but Leeds had a crucial match in hand.

Leeds took a giant step on 18 April by beating Ipswich, while Palace and Plymouth both drew, the Eagles 1-1 at home to West Brom. Then the following weekend saw a severe dent in Palace's hopes as they lost 2-0 at Brighton, while Plymouth won and Leeds drew. Palace were hanging in there, but failing to win in the last four matches looked likely to have cost them, as they next faced a tough match at home to third-placed Oldham, although their opponents' form had also deserted them at this crucial juncture.

Before that encounter, Leeds lost their match in hand at Reading, so four points now separated Plymouth in fourth and Palace in seventh, with Leeds and Ipswich sitting between the two. All had four matches left to play but Palace clearly had the toughest task in their next fixture. However, they shone on the day, defeating

Oldham 2-1, as Ipswich lost and Plymouth drew. Only Leeds matched Palace's result, beating Birmingham 4-0. The Eagles were now only two points away from a play-off place.

Oldham secured at least a play-off place by winning their next match, so there were now only two left up for grabs at the start of May. On 2 May, Derby achieved automatic promotion by beating Leeds, while Plymouth also lost. However, Palace failed to take advantage as they also suffered defeat, 1-0 at Sunderland. It was therefore a good day for Ipswich, who won at home to Blackburn. They and Leeds now occupied the two remaining play-off places, a point ahead of Plymouth and two clear of Palace.

Palace faced Portsmouth next, winning 1-0 thanks to an Ian Wright goal at Selhurst Park. Plymouth slipped up by losing at home, and Ipswich drew, but Leeds all but confirmed a play-off place with a victory at home to West Brom. With just one match remaining of the regular season, Palace needed to win at Hull and hope that Ipswich slipped up at home to Reading. Only a massive goal difference turnaround could prevent Leeds from finishing in the top five. Plymouth still entertained faint hopes but would need to win, while hoping that both Palace and Ipswich slipped up.

The final round of fixtures saw the Pilgrims defeated at Derby, while Leeds secured their place in the play-offs with victory at relegated Brighton. It was down to Palace and Ipswich. Palace had their chance, as Ipswich only took a point at home to Reading, while the Eagles were facing Hull, the team they had trounced 5-1 earlier in the season. It was a disastrous result for Palace, going down 3-0 at Boothferry Park against a team with nothing to play for. It left the Eagles in sixth place and cost them the opportunity of playing for a place back in the top tier as Leeds, Ipswich and Oldham joined Charlton Athletic in the end-of-season mini-tournament, the latter winning the final, ironically at Selhurst Park, to maintain their First Division status.

Things were clearly on the up for Palace, who had only just failed to make the play-offs in 1986/87, so surely the following season would provide an opportunity to finally make something of the 80s by achieving top-flight status. Or would it be heartbreak once again?

Palace's season started on 15 August 1987 with a 2-2 draw at Huddersfield, Mark Bright scoring twice for the Eagles. Next up were the team that had ruined Palace's play-off dreams a few months earlier, Hull City, at Selhurst Park. Palace were again thwarted, relying on two penalties to secure another 2-2 draw, hardly an inspiring start to the season. But worse was to come, as Palace then went down 2-1 at Barnsley to close out a disappointing month, sitting 19th in the table, still seeking their first win of the season.

This was to come on the very first day of the next month when they beat Middlesbrough 3-1 at home, Bright again scoring a double. And what a way to follow it up – a 6-0 thrashing of Birmingham City at

St Andrew's, a stunning performance that looked set to launch Palace's season. At home to West Brom, Palace found their goalscoring touch once more, winning 4-1, Mark Bright again scoring two, now partnering Ian Wright up front in what was looking like a lethal partnership. With three wins in a row, Palace had shot up to second in the table behind Barnsley.

Although not a rampant victory like the previous two, a fourth in a row, 2-1 at home to Leicester, took Palace to the top of the table, as Barnsley had been held at Aston Villa. The Eagles followed this with a 1-1 draw at Sheffield United, then a 3-2 win at Reading, before entering the League Cup in the second round, where they faced Fourth Division Newport County. Palace made easy work of the first leg at Selhurst Park, winning 4-0, Ian Wright scoring twice, so passage to the third round looked secure.

The following weekend saw Palace lose for the first time in eight matches when they went down 2-1 at home to Ipswich, and they failed to bounce back, losing their next match 2-0 at Shrewsbury. After such an exciting September, Palace had dropped to fourth in the table and couldn't afford to slip into a poor run, given that several teams were close on their heels. No such worries in the League Cup, though, where the Wright–Bright strike force gave them a 2-0 win at Newport.

The Eagles temporarily got back on track in the league, scoring the only goal at home to Millwall thanks to Mark Bright, but then suffered a heavy defeat at Aston

Villa, 4-1. One win in four meant Palace were now down to ninth, so their 2-1 victory at home to Swindon came as a welcome relief before the third round of the League Cup. Palace faced a tough task, however, drawn away at Manchester United, but putting up a good show in a 2-1 defeat. There was no such good performance to close out October, though, as Palace lost 2-0 at Bradford City, who were sitting pretty at the top of the table.

At the start of November, Mark Bright scored yet another double as Palace found their scoring boots again, winning 3-2 at Bournemouth, but they then failed to find the net in the Full Members Cup, losing to a single goal to First Division Oxford United in front of fewer than 1,500 fans. Bright and Wright were at it again the following weekend, scoring the goals in a 2-0 win at home to Stoke that saw Palace move up to fifth, but their away form was concerning, next losing 2-0 at Blackburn. Although Palace had won seven of nine matches at Selhurst Park, on the road they had only won three of ten, not the sort of form that would see them in the promotion places come the end of the season. But at least it was back to Selhurst Park at the end of the month, where Palace were still on good form, winning 3-0 against Leeds United.

Into December, and Palace at last found some good away form when beating sixth-placed Manchester City 3-1 at Maine Road, then continued their good home form by beating Sheffield United 2-1. Three wins on the bounce and suddenly they were back up to fourth and in the hunt for the top three automatic promotion places. Unfortunately, Hull City again put the kibosh on their hopes, beating them 2-1 at Boothferry Park, although it didn't affect Palace's league position.

Boxing Day saw Palace gain revenge for their earlier home defeat by Ipswich by winning 3-2 at Portman Road, this against a team sitting one place below them in the table, so a crucial three points that saw the Eagles move up to third. Then two days later, the scoreline was reversed at Selhurst Park as Palace went down 3-2 to Reading in a rare home defeat. More frustrating was the fact that Reading were bottom of the table, so it should have been an easy three points for Palace.

New Year's Day saw more revenge for Palace, this time beating Barnsley 3-2 at home. And the crazy fixture list saw them playing the next day, hitting four goals at Leicester, but unfortunately conceding the same number in a remarkable draw. Again this was lost points against a team that was bottom of the table before the match kicked off, but at least it was a point that saw Palace up to second, behind leaders Aston Villa. Going into 1988, the Eagles looked like strong candidates for promotion to the top tier at long last.

A week later saw Palace's FA Cup campaign kick off with a third-round tie at First Division Newcastle, another tough cup draw for the Eagles this season. Again it was a close affair, with Paul 'Gazza' Gascoigne's goal enough to seal Palace's fate, but at least leave them with promotion to concentrate on without the cup's distraction.

Their run-in started well, with a 2-1 home win over Huddersfield, finally managing to beat a team at the bottom of the table, albeit by a very narrow margin. But three points is three points, which was three more than they got next, losing 2-1 at Middlesbrough, who moved up to third in the table, one place behind Palace. In fact they managed to leapfrog them without playing, as Palace then lost 1-0 at Oldham, so Middlesbrough's slightly better goal difference saw them up to second, while the two teams just behind Palace, Millwall and Blackburn, had matches in hand. It could all easily unravel for Palace over the next few fixtures.

Blackburn won their match in hand to move second, then the next full round of fixtures saw Palace again beating Birmingham, this time 3-0 at Selhurst Park. To relieve the pressure somewhat, Millwall then lost their match in hand, so Palace were still in the promotion places with 13 matches left to play; still a long way to go. Disappointment came in a 1-0 defeat at West Brom, another team in the lower reaches of the league, and other results soon saw Palace down to fifth. A poor February ended with a home defeat, 2-1 to Shrewsbury. A month that had started with such promise of automatic promotion, now looked like being a battle for a play-off spot, as the Eagles slumped to sixth place.

March brought some cheer, though, as Palace beat Oldham 3-1 at home to stop the rot and move up a couple of places. Then a 1-1 draw at promotion rivals Millwall saw both teams drop two places to fifth and sixth, as Aston Villa, Blackburn, Middlesbrough and Bradford City occupied the top four places. These six looked odds-on to contest the fight for the top tier, with perhaps Leeds and Manchester City getting in on the act with a good run of form.

Palace faced one of those rivals, Bradford City, next but failed to make the most of their home advantage in a 1-1 draw that did a favour for the other promotion hopefuls. It was another draw for Palace, 2-2 away at Swindon, that saw them losing pace with the top two of Aston Villa and Blackburn, so it now looked like automatic promotion was out of the picture, while Leeds had also joined the play-off contention.

April began well for Palace, winning 3-0 at home to Bournemouth, on a day when rivals Bradford City and Leeds both lost, but they failed to take advantage of this when drawing 1-1 at Stoke, while Bradford City won. Palace were sixth, two points behind Bradford City but four ahead of Leeds, so a play-off place was still realistic, with only five matches remaining. However, next for Palace it was league leaders Aston Villa, although Leeds also faced a tough match at home to second-placed Millwall. Leeds lost, but Palace's draw against Villa saw them fall further behind the play-off places, as Bradford City won.

At the top of the table, what had looked a forgone conclusion for Villa and Blackburn had been turned on its head. Villa had won just one in five, while Blackburn had also been on a poor run. It was now Millwall at the top, with Middlesbrough second, followed by Blackburn, Villa and Bradford City. Palace were in sixth, but now four points adrift of the all-important fifth place, with only four matches left to play. Bradford City then moved up to second with a win over Reading, leaving Palace five points of fifth place, although having a match in hand over Aston Villa.

On the day that Liverpool were yet again crowned champions of the First Division, Palace kept their hopes of joining them in the top tier next season alive by beating Plymouth 3-1 away. Aston Villa also won, but the Eagles now had just three points between them and the play-off places, as Blackburn were down to fifth. Blackburn then drew their match in hand, so it was Middlesbrough's turn to occupy the last play-off place, three points above Palace. Only Millwall of the top six seemed capable of maintaining a winning run at this stage, so the remaining promotion places were clearly up for grabs over the remaining few weeks.

Palace did themselves a massive favour on the last day of April by defeating rivals Blackburn 2-0 at Selhurst Park. It didn't help their league position but they were now only one point behind their opponents of the day and had a vastly superior goal difference. Meanwhile, Millwall continued their excellent run with a win to secure at least a play-off spot, and Bradford City and Middlesbrough also took three points. The top six had now all played 42 of their 44 matches, so Palace would need one of them to slip up in the remaining two fixtures to stand any chance of making a bid for the First Division.

It also meant that the Eagles ideally needed to win both remaining matches, but on 2 May they lost 2-0 at Leeds to severely dent their ambitions. On this same day, Millwall became champions, while Aston Villa, Bradford City and Middlesbrough all secured play-off places, and all could still finish runners-up. While the Eagles were coming away from Elland Road empty-handed, Blackburn were struggling to a draw at home to relation-threatened Reading; however, it could be a crucial point, as Blackburn were now two points clear of Palace, who would definitely need to win their final fixture, and hope that Blackburn failed to win.

Palace faced Manchester City at home, while Blackburn were away at champions Millwall. The fixtures favoured Palace, but it perhaps depended on whether the champions were in party mode, although Manchester City also had nothing to play for. On 7 May, Palace did everything asked of them, defeating City 2-0 in front of Selhurst Park's largest gate of the season, 17,555. Unfortunately, the fears that the Lions may not be up for the fight were not unfounded, as Blackburn took Millwall apart in a 4-1 victory at The Den.

For the second season in a row, Palace had been thwarted at the last, finishing sixth again, two points away from a place in the play-offs. For the record, Aston Villa finished runners-up to Millwall to take the second automatic promotion place, while Middlesbrough,

Bradford City and Blackburn Rovers entered the play-offs against Chelsea. These kicked off the day after Wimbledon, under Dave Bassett, had shocked Liverpool and ruined their double hopes by winning the FA Cup at Wembley, 1-0. Middlesbrough beat Chelsea in the play-off final to secure top-flight status.

Chapter 11

Better Late than Never

AFTER TWO seasons of finishing just one place out of the play-offs, Steve Coppell's men looked to make it third time lucky in 1988/89. Although the Team of the 80s hadn't lived up to expectations, could they at least finish the decade on a high by achieving that all-important promotion and spending the final season of the 80s in the First Division?

The league season started on 27 August 1988, although Palace had to wait three days to kick off their campaign, drawing 1-1 at home to relegated Chelsea. It became an inauspicious start to Palace's drive for promotion, as they next went down 2-0 at home to Watford, played out a goalless draw at Walsall, a 1-1 home draw with Shrewsbury, and 1-1 draws at Sunderland and Portsmouth. Hardly the stuff of champions: six matches, no wins, only five points on the board and sitting 20th in the table.

A victory finally came, but it was in the first leg of the second round of the League Cup, 2-1 at fellow second-tier Swindon, Bright and Wright scoring the Palace goals. Perhaps this energised the Eagles, as they next achieved their first league victory of the season in style, beating Plymouth 4-1 at Selhurst Park. That momentum was then maintained in a 2-0 home win over Ipswich, Wright and Bright again providing the goals to take Palace up to mid-table respectability.

Next came an amazing match at Blackburn, where Palace came out on the wrong side of a nine-goal thriller, 5-4 to the home team. The Eagles progressed in the League Cup, beating Swindon 2-0 in the home leg to move into the third round. Back in the league they grabbed their first away win of the season, 1-0 at Bradford City, Ian Wright scoring the all-important goal against strong opponents. Then came another team that had proved tricky over the past couple of seasons, but this time Palace had no problem in defeating Hull City 3-1 at home. From a poor start, they now had four wins from the last five matches and had moved up to eighth in the table, having a match in hand over most of those above them.

Another home win, 1-0 over Oxford, showed that Palace could be serious contenders come the end of the season in what looked a tough league, with Watford, Manchester City, Blackburn and Portsmouth all having made good starts to the campaign, and the likes of Chelsea and Ipswich not far behind.

Palace's great run came to an end at Stoke City, losing 2-1 at the end of October. Then, worse still, came a 4-1 drubbing at Third Division Bristol City in the League Cup to end any hopes of a decent run in the competition. A 1-1 home draw with Barnsley and a 2-0 defeat at Bournemouth did nothing to improve the mood, as Palace dropped to 11th in the table. However, the gloom was finally lifted by a 4-2 home win over Leicester, before Palace entered the Full Members Cup to defeat Walsall by the same scoreline at Selhurst Park.

The goals were beginning to flow again, and this continued at West Brom, Palace scoring three; however, the Baggies managed five in another high-scoring match. Then the goals dried up in a goalless encounter at home to Manchester City, leaving Palace 13th in the table, falling off the pace. Unusually, Palace only scored one goal against Birmingham, a team they had a habit of thrashing, but it was enough to take all three points at St Andrew's.

The Full Members Cup wasn't a competition that Palace had much joy with but they came away from The Dell having beaten Southampton 2-1 to take a notable scalp, as the Saints were sitting sixth in the First Division. But for some reason Palace couldn't transfer this form to the league, drawing 0-0 at home to Leeds just before Christmas. The Boxing Day fixture brought the old rivalry with Brighton, who were the happier of the two after winning 3-1 in front of a big crowd at the Goldstone Ground to push Palace down to 14th. Four days later there was a bit of Christmas cheer as Palace got back to winning ways by beating Oldham 3-2 at Boundary Park.

New Year saw Palace reach the halfway point in the season with an impressive 4-0 win over Walsall, Mark Bright hitting a hat-trick. The half-term report would read 'must do better', as Palace were eighth in the table, but a continuation of their inconsistent form would not see them challenge for the play-offs or automatic promotion. However, they were only six points off fifth place, so a decent second half to the season could change everything.

That would have to wait, though, as the third round of the FA Cup beckoned, Palace drawn at Second Division Stoke City. It was another disappointing exit for the Eagles, going down 1-0 to spoil any hopes of a trip to Wembley. The Full Members Cup was still bringing joy, however, Palace beating another First Division team, Luton, by a superb 4-1 scoreline at Selhurst Park.

Away from the cups, in a tough league encounter at second-placed Chelsea, Palace lost to the only goal but then won 2-1 at home to Swindon before playing in the quarter-final of the Full Members Cup. Again Palace got the better of top-tier opponents, this time beating Middlesbrough 3-2 at Ayresome Park, a team sitting a comfortable tenth in the First Division. Palace were once again proving that they could mix it with the big teams, but first needed to improve their league form so that they could get the opportunity to do that week in, week out in the top division.

They improved their chances of this at the start of February by winning 2-1 at Ipswich, Ian Wright bagging both goals. It was a victory that took the Eagles above their opponents and into sixth place. The Wright–Bright combination was then on target again, but their goals weren't enough to beat Blackburn in a 2-2 draw at Selhurst Park. Palace then had a gap of a couple of weeks before exiting the Full Members Cup at the semi-final stage, 3-1 at First Division Nottingham Forest. It had been a good run in which the Eagles had given a very good account of themselves, but they were to miss out on the chance to play in the final at Wembley.

With only the league left to play for, Palace continued their decent run with a 2-0 win over Bradford City, Mark Bright scoring both goals. However, a 1-0 loss at Oxford showed that Palace still sometimes struggled against teams in the lower half of the table, something they couldn't afford to do in what was left of the season. It became two defeats in a row when they went down 3-2 at home to Bournemouth, one of their main promotion rivals, who were sitting fifth, with Palace dropping to 12th. The poor run was somewhat stopped with a 1-1 draw at Barnsley but Palace looked to be dropping out of the race for promotion at this stage, although still with 15 matches left to play.

A Mark Bright penalty was enough to secure a home win over Sunderland, before Palace took an excellent three points with another single-goal victory, at Watford. Next up the Seagulls, and Palace avenged their Boxing

Day defeat with a 2-1 win at Selhurst Park. Three wins and suddenly Palace were back in the hunt, given their three matches in hand over most of their rivals. However, it was all spoiled by another one of those performances against lesser opposition, Shrewsbury, who had a habit of taking points off Palace and did so again by beating them 2-1 at Gay Meadow.

The Eagles bounced back well, though, winning 2-1 at Leeds at the beginning of April, then 2-0 at home to Oldham three days later. With matches to catch up, Palace were soon back in action, again beating bogey team Hull City, this time 1-0 away. Then on the day of the terrible events at Hillsborough in the FA Cup semi-final between Liverpool and Nottingham Forest, Palace scored their fourth win in a row, 2-0 against Portsmouth. On a day when the game of football was secondary, Palace found themselves up in fourth place and among the promotion candidates, still with a couple of matches in hand.

Coming into the final weeks of the season there were still several teams contending for automatic promotion and the play-offs. The top two would be promoted automatically, while the next four would contend the play-offs at the end of the season. Chelsea achieved promotion early by beating Leeds at Stamford Bridge, but there were eight or nine other teams vying for the opportunity to get into the top tier. Palace were well in the hunt, doing themselves a favour with a 2-0 win at Plymouth, thanks to a double by Mark Bright, but then they lost 1-0 at Swindon, one of their promotion rivals, three days later. They now only had one match in hand and had just missed the opportunity to move up to third.

In a full league programme the following weekend, Palace beat West Brom 1-0 at home with an Ian Wright goal, while Manchester City secured at least a play-off place by beating Oxford. The Second Division teams were all in action again on 1 May, Palace securing a 1-1 draw at Manchester City, a good result, but only one point. Of their main rivals, Watford lost but Blackburn, West Brom, Barnsley and Swindon all won to keep the pressure on at the top. At least Palace knew they wouldn't have to face Shrewsbury next season as they were relegated after losing to Swindon.

All the play-off candidates had two more matches to play, apart from Palace, who had three. Watford, Palace and Blackburn all had 74 points and were sitting in that order on goal difference. Swindon were just two points behind, while West Brom and Barnsley were still mathematically in the hunt, but would need to win both matches and hope other results went their way.

Next up for Palace was Leicester away, a team with nothing to play for, but they fought out a 2-2 draw at Filbert Street, the Eagles relying on two penalties to secure a single point. But it was a point that was enough for Palace to be assured of a play-off place. Meanwhile, Manchester City secured the runners-up spot with a draw of their own, so the Eagles now needed to look for a third-place finish so they would face the team finishing sixth, the supposedly easier of the semi-finals.

Their match in hand was against another mid-table team, Stoke City, at home. Another penalty was enough to take the vital three points, so Palace had moved up to third. Their final position was now in their own hands as they faced Birmingham City, a team they had a great recent record against. However, they would need to win to be absolutely certain of third place.

The final fixtures were played on 13 May, and it was another emphatic win over the Blues for Palace, 4-1, Ian Wright taking the glory with a hat-trick. For a change, the other results were irrelevant; Palace had finished third in the Second Division, behind Chelsea and Manchester City. They would now face Swindon in one play-off semi-final, while Watford and Blackburn would face off in the other, the ties to be played over two legs, with the final to also be played over two legs rather than currently, when the final leads to a nice Wembley day out.

While Blackburn and Watford played out a goalless draw at Ewood Park, it was first blood to Swindon against Palace at the County Ground, where the home team scored the only goal (actually a Jeff Hopkins own goal) to take an advantage to Selhurst Park. Swindon had dominated the match, so Palace knew they would be in for a real battle at home in the return leg three days later.

A huge turnout led to a delayed kick-off but Palace were soon ahead after Mark Bright's eighth-minute goal levelled up the aggregate scores. Just before half-time Palace took the lead in the tie with a goal by Bright's partner, Ian Wright. There were no further goals, and Palace had made it to the final, where they would face Blackburn, who had squeaked through after drawing 1-1 after extra time against Watford, to go through on the away goals rule.

While Palace were probably deemed to be favourites to win the final, having finished above Blackburn in the league, the head-to-heads during the season were in Blackburn's favour, Rovers having won that astonishing encounter at Ewood Park 5-4 and gained a 2-2 draw at Selhurst Park. It looked like being a close-run thing, probably coming down to a shoot-out between two deadly marksmen, Simon Garner for Blackburn and Ian Wright for Palace, who between them had scored over 50 goals in the league and cups in 1988/89. Either that or their backups, Howard Gayle and Mark Bright, who had both scored over 20 goals.

The first leg was played on 31 May 1989 at Ewood Park, and it was first blood to the home team when Gayle scored the opener on 21 minutes. Just six minutes later Palace looked to be in big trouble when Gayle made it two, as Blackburn dominated proceedings in the first half. The second half didn't see much improvement for Palace, and they looked doomed when Jeff Hopkins felled the dangerous Gayle in the penalty area and the referee pointed to the spot. Surely 3-0 would be too much to come back from, even with a second leg at home to follow. Howard Gayle stepped up to take the penalty, the opportunity for his hat-trick, only to put the ball wide of the post. A real let-off for Palace, with 20 minutes remaining.

The remaining action all came in the final few minutes of the match – first Palace giving themselves hope with an Eddie McGoldrick goal on 86 minutes but Blackburn hitting back in the final minutes when Simon Garner made it 3-1 and advantage Blackburn.

Three days later the teams met at Selhurst Park, with Palace knowing they must score first to have any chance of winning the final. Over 26,000 fans watched as Blackburn started the match on the front foot and looked likely to add to their two-goal advantage. However, Palace settled into the match and it was Ian Wright who fired home in the 17th minute to reduce the overall arrears to a single goal. He then came close twice more in the first half, but at the break Blackburn still led 3-2 on aggregate. Palace had just 45 minutes to turn it around.

Just two minutes into the second half it was Blackburn's turn to concede a penalty; this for a foul on McGoldrick. David Madden made no mistake from the spot to level the tie at 3-3. Neither team looked like finding the net in the remaining 43 minutes, so extra time beckoned. It looked like going the distance as the clocked ticked down to three minutes remaining. Then, with perfect timing, Ian Wright got his second goal of the match when he headed home from McGoldrick's cross, leaving Blackburn hardly any time to recover. Rovers couldn't muster anything, and it was Palace who celebrated promotion with a thrilling 4-3 aggregate victory, after all appeared lost in the first leg. The Team of the 80s were at last due to produce a fitting finale to the decade, playing its final season, 1989/90, back in the First Division and achieving a dream of reaching a Wembley cup final.

Chapter 12
We're on Our Way to Wembley

HAVING ACHIEVED promotion through the play-offs the previous season, there was to be no repeat of Palace's table-topping performance from a decade earlier. This was to be a season of consolidation in the top tier. Rather that than become a yo-yo club between the First and Second Divisions, but it would require more consistency than Palace had shown over the previous few seasons.

Palace's season kicked off, ironically, against old rivals QPR, now managed by Trevor Francis, England's first £1m footballer, and including Kenny Sansom in their line-up. Wright scored both goals in a 2-0 victory, but unfortunately for Palace the goalscorer was Paul Wright of QPR. On this opening day, Manchester United had thumped Arsenal 4-1, so were a daunting opponent for Palace in their next match, at Selhurst Park. This time Ian Wright did score in a decent 1-1 draw against strong opponents.

Palace were at home again the following weekend but disappointingly went down 1-0 to Coventry City, a team they would have expected to beat. Not a great start to the season, with the Eagles already second from bottom with just one point to their name, and Wimbledon up next. This time it was success at Selhurst Park, as Palace took all three points with a 2-0 win, Wright on the scoresheet again.

Next came a match that Palace fans will want to forget but that probably still haunts many. The Eagles travelled to Anfield to face Liverpool on 12 September, a team that included the attacking force of John Barnes, Ian Rush and Peter Beardsley. Palace actually started the match quite well and Geoff Thomas hit the post when the score was 1-0, but what followed was an avalanche of goals as Liverpool hit a further eight without reply, five of them in the second half. They were even able to bring the departing John Aldridge off the bench to score a penalty in front of the Kop on his last performance for the Reds. Meanwhile, at 6-0 Palace missed a spot kick of their own through Thomas, but it wouldn't have made much difference on the night.

After a result like that it would have been easy, even at this early stage, for Palace's season to capitulate, but this team was built of sterner stuff than the young players of the early 80s. A tough match at The Dell saw them gain a well-earned point in a 1-1 draw, before they entered the League Cup in the second round, First Division teams receiving a bye through to this stage. In the first leg Palace were on the end of a minor giant-killing as they went down 2-1 to Leicester of the Second

Division. Dreams of a Wembley visit already looked to be fading in this competition.

Back in the league, Palace were again at home, and gained their second win of the season, 1-0 over Nottingham Forest, Ian Wright hitting the winner. In a strange balance of fixtures, it was back toSelhurst Park the following weekend, where Palace did the job again, this time over Everton, 2-1, that man Wright scoring yet again in his impressive start to the season. By the end of September, Palace were now up to a creditable ninth in the table, as Liverpool led the way.

Wembley dreams were reignited a few days later when Palace pulled off a 3-2 win at Leicester to leave the aggregate score at 4-4. However, Palace's three away goals proved the difference as they moved into the third round.

Finally playing another away fixture in the league, the Eagles then came unstuck at Derby County, going down 3-1, but followed it up with another good result at home, beating Millwall 4-3, with two apiece from the Wright–Bright combo. After this goal fest came a goalless draw at home to Nottingham Forest in the third round of the League Cup before a return to league action, where Palace's away form was a cause for concern. Strong at home, having won four and drawn one of their six matches, on their travels the Eagles were yet to win and had gained only one point in five matches following their 2-1 defeat at Aston Villa.

Then came another drubbing away from home, this in the League Cup replay where Palace shipped five goals without reply at Nottingham Forest to exit the competition. This poor away form continued the following weekend when Manchester City, who had been struggling, beat Palace 3-0 to move above them in the table, the Eagles now sitting 15th and slipping towards the relegation places.

Despite having been strong at Selhurst Park, Palace only managed a 1-1 draw with Luton, then lost 3-2 to Spurs. Worryingly, the goals of Ian Wright had dried up, and all three goals from these two home matches came from Mark Bright. Also of concern was the slide that Palace were on after a decent start to the league campaign, as they were now only one point above the relegation fight. One of those struggling clubs was bottom-placed Sheffield Wednesday, where Palace played next, gaining a 2-2 draw, which was of little use to either team.

The Full Members Cup was still going, and Palace gained a much-needed morale boost as they beat Luton 4-1 at home but, more importantly, Sheffield Wednesday then pulled off a shock 2-0 victory over league leaders Liverpool, so Palace were now only one point off the bottom of the table. And it got worse, as the Eagles next went down 3-0 at home to QPR at the start of December, as home form also began to desert them.

Then came Palace's best performance of the season so far, as they went to Old Trafford and came away with their first win on the road, as two Bright goals secured a 2-1 win over Manchester United. This was a major boost leading into the busy Christmas and New Year period, and they followed it up with their second away win, beating Charlton 2-1. Two away wins on the trot meant the Eagles had flown up the table to 12th. They then beat the same opponents in the Full Members Cup, 2-0 at Selhurst Park. Not an important competition but three wins in a row is always good for the confidence.

On Boxing Day, Palace faced Chelsea at home, drawing 2-2, with Ian Wright scoring his first goal for quite some time to help secure a point. Just four days later Palace were in action at Selhurst Park again, beating Norwich 1-0, with Wright now back in the groove with the crucial goal. However, New Year's Day saw Palace heavily beaten, 4-1 at high-flying Arsenal, to bring their recent unbeaten run to an end before the start of their FA Cup campaign. Here they faced Portsmouth at home, and came through a tough encounter 2-1 to move into the fourth round.

Coventry City completed a double over Palace the following weekend, winning 1-0 at Highfield Park, before the Eagles faced the daunting prospect of Liverpool again, but at least they had home advantage this time. The previous mauling at Anfield didn't deter the fans either, as nearly 30,000 turned up to see the Reds triumph 2-0.

Palace had a nice draw in the FA Cup, at home to Third Division Huddersfield, and they made no mistake, winning 4-0, to move into the fifth round. However, league form wasn't as good, the Eagles going down

3-1 at Nottingham Forest, to reawaken the threat of relegation. Although Charlton were well adrift at the bottom, Palace were now only two points ahead of the bottom three. Somewhat surprisingly, Alex Ferguson's Manchester United were now one place below them in 17th. Palace did themselves a big favour the following weekend, beating Southampton 3-1 at Selhurst Park, as they and Manchester United both jumped up a few places.

Although Palace had previously seen little success in the Full Members Cup, and the fans had shown little interest, this season they had reached the semi-finals of the South region, where they faced Swindon Town of the Second Division. A single goal was all that was needed to take Palace to the final. However, the important cup competition was up next, the fifth round of the FA Cup, where Palace had drawn Fourth Division Rochdale, one of two fourth-tier teams to reach the last 16. At Selhurst Park, surely Palace would ease through, but it was a close-run thing as the Eagles took the honours 1-0 to move into the quarter-finals. Dreams of a Wembley cup final were becoming real. But in the Full Members Cup Final South, it wasn't Wembley that beckoned, it was Selhurst Park, as Palace faced Chelsea. However, home advantage counted for nothing as the Blues triumphed 2-0 in the first leg.

Still needing points to secure top-tier football for another season, Palace gained one in a 1-1 draw at home to Sheffield Wednesday, a disappointing result against a team on the same number of points. However, three valuable points were gained at White Hart Lane, as an Alan Pardew goal separated the teams, a great win against a Spurs team that was sixth in the table and included Gary Lineker and Paul Gascoigne.

In March, Palace faced the other Fourth Division team that had been on a great run in the FA Cup, Cambridge United. The Eagles were perhaps getting the luck of the draw, but Cambridge had hit five goals past Third Division Bristol City in the second replay of the previous round and had Dion Dublin up front, so could turn out to be difficult opponents at their Abbey Stadium. And so it turned out, but Geoff Thomas's goal from a mishit shot was enough to see Palace through to the semi-final, where they would be facing, guess who … Liverpool, who had already hit 11 goals past them this season.

There was to be no success in the Full Members Cup, though, as Chelsea confirmed a 4-0 aggregate victory by winning 2-0 at Stamford Bridge. One dream of a Wembley cup final had gone for the Eagles. Then 4-0 was the scoreline in the Palace's next league match, as they were heavily beaten at Everton and now needed to ensure that thoughts weren't focused too much on the FA Cup, as points were still needed to avoid slipping into an end-of-season fight for First Division survival.

A useful point was gained at home to Derby in a 1-1 draw, although perhaps it was two points lost against a mid-table team. Worse still, Ian Wright suffered a broken leg that would put him out for all but the last match of the season. Palace's next result was a superb win, beating top-of-the-table Aston Villa 1-0 at Selhurst Park to dent their title bid. Next was bottom-of-the-table Millwall at The Den, and again Palace took all three points, winning 2-1. They now had 40 points and, barring an awful run to the end of the season, looked safe for another season of top-tier football.

After two wins, Palace then slipped up away at Norwich, 2-0, a team going well in seventh place, but maybe Palace had one eye on their next match, the FA Cup semi-final against Liverpool at Villa Park on 8 April 1990, a date that will remain in Palace fans' memories for a very long time.

On a sunny day at Villa Park it was Liverpool who started strongly. After just 14 minutes Steve McMahon set up Ian Rush, who took the ball past keeper Nigel Martyn and slid home the opening goal of the semi-final. However, Rush was to only last half an hour before succumbing to a rib injury. With John Aldridge having moved to play in Spain, they had no natural backup, so John Barnes moved into a central striking role, with left-back Steve Staunton now playing on the left wing. Despite this setback, Liverpool continued to dominate the first-half possession, but were not creating chances to add to their early lead. It remained 1-0 at half-time.

This was the first time that both FA Cup semi-finals were being televised live, and the BBC had enlisted none other than Malcolm Allison to give his views during the match. At half-time he said that, although Liverpool were technically the better team, Palace were physically stronger and needed to go for it a bit more. Prophetic words indeed.

Liverpool were forced in to a second change during the break as Gary Gillespie had a groin strain and was unable to continue. The Reds had now used both substitutes with 45 minutes (at least) still to play. This could prove to be crucial.

An incredible start to the second half saw Palace equalise after just 17 seconds, as McMahon gave the ball away from the restart. John Pemberton intercepted his pass and set off down the right, outpacing David Burrows and Ronnie Whelan. He crossed the ball, which fell to John Salako, who hit a volley towards goal. Liverpool's keeper Bruce Grobbelaar saved with his feet but could only direct the ball straight to Mark Bright, who volleyed a shot that found the net, despite McMahon's valiant effort to make up for his earlier error. Palace were back in the match.

Play settled down after the electric start to the second half, with Liverpool reasserting a level of control, but then on 70 minutes Palace turned the match on its head. They were awarded a free kick after Alan Hansen fouled Bright 35 yards from the Liverpool goal. Andy Gray sent in a curling cross and Bright again got the better of Hansen in the air. The ball dropped to Gary O'Reilly, who hit a shot that beat Grobbelaar and flew into the top-right corner of the net. It was O'Reilly's first goal for the club, who were now just 20 minutes from Wembley.

Time ticked on as Liverpool sought the equaliser, but Palace were hanging in there. However, there was still time for plenty of drama. With just nine minutes remaining the scores were level again when McMahon atoned for his earlier mistake that let Palace back into the match. Venison took the ball to the byline, then pulled it back to McMahon, who was unmarked just inside the penalty area. He opened up his body to send a shot into the top-right corner for a brilliant goal. Perhaps Palace fans were now fearing the inevitable.

And just one minute later those fears were realised when Liverpool were awarded a penalty. Almost from the restart the Reds went in search of the winner, Beardsley setting off on a run down the left. He flicked the ball to Staunton, who charged into the penalty area and was brought down clumsily by Pemberton. The ref pointed to the spot. Barnes coolly slotted home the penalty to give Liverpool a 3-2 lead with just a few minutes remaining.

It now looked all over for valiant Palace, with the inevitability of a Liverpool victory and yet another cup final for the Reds. But the Eagles weren't done yet. As 'You'll Never Walk Alone' reverberated around the stadium, and the Liverpool fans began to plan their trip to Wembley, Palace struck an unlikely equaliser with just two minutes to play. It was all a bit of a mess, but they all count, as they say. Grobbelaar came out to punch clear a long, desperate punt forward by Andy Thorn, but the keeper didn't get enough distance on his clearance. The ball found the head of Geoff Thomas, who headed towards goal, with Grobbelaar now stranded in no-man's land. Meanwhile, Staunton had got back to cover the goal and blocked the header with his chest, but his clearance only sent the ball up into the air towards Gray. He looped a header goalwards, and time seemed to stand still … as the ball found the top of the goal and Palace were level at 3-3 in this incredible match.

Liverpool's back line, usually so calm and assured, had been given a hard time by the Palace strikers, and this goal typified the inexplicable panic that seemed to set in at the heart of the Reds' defence during this match. However, their real danger was their strike force, and they very nearly won the match in the final minute when Barnes moved in from the right and curled a low shot goalwards that Nigel Martyn did well to keep out. But the Liverpool defenders still had time to give Palace one last chance to snatch a winner when Glenn Hysén gave away a needless free kick for a foul on Bright. Gray again curled in a free kick that caused mayhem in the Liverpool defence, who all stood like statues as Thorn won a header that hit the bar. Barnes, back to defend the free kick, headed the ball behind for a corner, but Palace's last chance had gone, and the semi-final moved into extra time.

Just two minutes into the added 30 minutes, Staunton had a golden opportunity to put Liverpool back in front as he raced through on goal with only Martyn to beat. This was where he showed he was really a full-back, not a striker, as he lashed his shot over the bar to let Palace off the hook.

Although Liverpool were on top during the first half of extra time, it was Palace who found the net with two minutes remaining; however, it didn't count. Salako crossed from the left, Grobbelaar came out to claim it but misjudged the flight, as Gray and Hysén got in a tangle. In another farcical piece of defending the ball was heading towards the Liverpool goal, where Hansen's attempt to hook it away only succeeded in putting the ball into his own net. Unfortunately, the ref adjudged the challenge by Gray on Hysén to be a foul, so the goal didn't stand. However, Liverpool's defensive calamities must have given Palace confidence that any ball sent into their penalty area would cause problems.

The second period of extra time revealed two tired teams who had given everything in the first scintillating 90 minutes, until Palace suddenly found a burst of energy that was to prove crucial in sealing their Wembley final place. Thorn hit a long pass down their left, where the ever-dangerous Bright again got the better of Hysén and won a corner. Once again, an opportunity to send the ball into a dangerous area. And so it proved, as the ball was swung in towards the near post, where Thorn flicked it on. Alan Pardew came through a pack of players to power a header past the keeper to put Palace 4-3 ahead with just 11 minutes remaining.

Liverpool inevitably poured forward in search of the equaliser, and Palace had Martyn to thank for them not getting one. Ray Houghton got to the byline and put in a cross to the far post where Barnes jumped high to head the ball down towards goal. Martyn had scrambled back and not only pulled off the save but held on to the ball, with Red shirts waiting to pounce. It was Liverpool's last chance, and the ref's whistle for full time shortly afterwards brought a huge roar from the Palace fans and relief for their tired players. However, they still had the energy to enjoy their celebrations on the pitch in front of their joyous fans. Steve Coppell was probably the calmest person around, joking that he was panicking that they hadn't booked the hotel in case of a replay. But there was not any need for that – Crystal Palace were going to Wembley to play in the FA Cup Final for the first time in their 85-year history.[7]

On the same day, Coppell's old club Manchester United also fought out a 3-3 draw in the other semi-final, against Oldham of the Second Division. The teams couldn't be separated after extra time, so it went to a replay three days later, which United won 2-1 at Maine Road. However, this wasn't the mighty Manchester United that was to come in the Premier League years. They were one place below Palace in the table and the Eagles had already beaten them earlier in the season, so hopes must have been high for a first major trophy for the cabinet at Selhurst Park.

---

7   Scott Murray. 'Crystal Palace 4-3 Liverpool: 1990 FA Cup semi-final – as it happened', *The Guardian*. 8 April 2020.

The following weekend saw Palace back in league action, where they drew 1-1 at home with Arsenal, a result that saw them slip below both Manchester clubs, but still seven points above the danger zone. Just two days later they were in action again, going down to a heavy defeat, 3-0 at Chelsea. Any concerns that the cup final would lead to a complete drop-off in league form were dispelled, though, when Palace beat relegation-threatened Charlton 2-0 at Selhurst Park, a result that ensured Palace would play First Division football next season.

A 1-0 defeat at Kenilworth Road to Luton Town followed but wasn't important at this stage, although good form leading up to the cup final would be great for confidence. This was achieved with a 1-0 win at Wimbledon, who were doing well in eighth place in the table, then a 2-2 draw at home to Manchester City in the final match of the season. Palace had finished 15th in the table on the same points as the two Manchester clubs but with an inferior goal difference, largely thanks to some heavy defeats. Their semi-final victims, Liverpool, won the league title at a gallop, nine points clear of Aston Villa.

That was all academic, however, as 12 May saw the FA Cup Final at Wembley in front of 80,000 people, with Palace not only looking for their first major trophy, but also a first time in European competition the following season. Interestingly, this was the last FA Cup Final to be played between two teams with all-

British line-ups. Palace's team was all English, with Ian Wright recovering from his broken leg in time to make the bench:

> Nigel Martyn, John Pemberton, Richard Shaw, Andy Gray, Gary O'Reilly, Andy Thorn, Phil Barber, Geoff Thomas (c), Mark Bright, John Salako, Alan Pardew.
> Subs: Ian Wright and David Madden.

Manchester United lined up with eight English, two Scottish and one Welsh player, with further representatives from England and Wales on the bench:

> Jim Leighton, Paul Ince, Lee Martin, Steve Bruce, Mike Phelan, Gary Pallister, Bryan Robson (c), Neil Webb, Brian McClair, Mark Hughes, Danny Wallace.
> Subs: Mark Robins and Clayton Blackmore.

This was the first FA Cup Final to be played in front of an all-seater crowd and would see the winner play in the 1990/91 European Cup Winners' Cup, as the ban on English clubs in European competition had just been lifted. While, apart from the semi-final, Palace had enjoyed a comfortable cup draw on their way to Wembley, Manchester United had become the first team to reach the final after playing all their ties away from home, defeating Nottingham Forest, Hereford United,

Newcastle United and Sheffield United before the semi-final triumph over Oldham.

The semi-finals had seen 13 goals scored, and the final didn't disappoint on the goalscoring front either. First blood went to Palace on 17 minutes when O'Reilly headed home Barber's free kick via the head of Pallister to send the Eagles' fans wild with delight. On 35 minutes it was level when McClair got free down United's right wing and put a cross in for Robson to head towards goal. This one took a deflection on its way in too, off Pemberton's leg, to evade Martyn in the Palace goal. No further goals came the first half, but the drama was not yet over.

Just after the hour mark, United took the lead when a cross-cum-shot by Webb reached Hughes, who fired low into the goal. Just seven minutes later Ian Wright was introduced to the fray in place of Phil Barber, with Palace in need of his goalscoring touch. It didn't take long for him to make an impact. Three minutes after coming on, he went on a run that took him past Phelan and Pallister before shooting past Leighton to level things up at 2-2. Although there were still over 20 minutes to play, there were no further goals, the closest call being a Phelan shot that hit the Palace bar.

In extra time it was that man Wright again, giving Palace the lead two minutes into the added period. Leighton hesitated to come out for a Salako cross, leaving Wright to volley home for 3-2. It stayed that way for the rest of the first half and well into the second period of extra time. Palace were just two minutes from glory when Wallace threaded through a pass for Hughes to run on to. The Welsh striker calmly slid the ball past Martyn to leave the final score at 3-3. So close for Palace but it would be a replay five days later, again at Wembley.

It was a completely different affair in the replay from the goal fests of the semi-finals and final, with just a single goal dividing the teams in an uneventful match. Unfortunately, the goal was scored by Martin of United, who took home the trophy and sealed a place in the European Cup Winners' Cup, which they would go on to win in 1990/91. Palace went home empty-handed, having missed their opportunity of silverware in the first match.

Chapter 13

What Went Wrong?

IT'S NOW over 40 years since Crystal Palace FC were given the tag of the Team of the 80s, and it proved to be a heavy burden indeed. From briefly shining at the top of the First Division, to several years in the second tier and even sliding into the third tier, the dream turned into a nightmare for Palace supporters, who only got to celebrate in the final year of a decade that their team were expected to rule.

With thrilling players such as Kenny Sansom, Vince Hilaire and ex-England captain Gerry Francis in their ranks, Palace looked destined to challenge the big boys in the top tier for years to come, particularly after winning the FA Youth Cup two years in succession and building an academy that was the envy of all around. Articles have been written and even a documentary made about the Team of the 80s, but there are many reasons why things didn't work out as anticipated, and as Jimmy Greaves famously quipped, 'Football's a funny old game.'

Unfortunately, as often happens with so-called 'smaller' teams, they need to sell to survive, and Palace were no different, Kenny Sansom's transfer to Arsenal a case in point. Sansom went on to have an incredible career with club and country, undeniably one of England's best left-backs of all time, gaining 86 caps. What if he had stayed at Palace? Having made his debut at 16 for the Eagles, what a difference he could have made as he gained experience and became the great player he did. But he was sold in 1980 for £1m plus Clive Allen going in the opposite direction, in what turned out to be a bargain for the Gunners. Sold just as Palace were looking to make their mark. Even worse, apparently it was against the player's wishes, as he wanted to stay at Selhurst Park ... but money talks.

Then there was Vince Hilaire, a truly gifted individual, who was only one year older than Sansom when he made his Palace debut in 1977. He had come through the youth ranks at Palace under Malcolm Allison and was part of the youth team that reached the semi-finals of the FA Youth Cup in 1975/76, before winning it in 1976/77. He stayed at Palace until 1984, but by then they were struggling and, after 255 appearances for the club, Hilaire was on his way, never to reach the heights he promised, and failing to gain even one senior international cap. And then there was the colour of his skin. As a prominent Black footballer, Hilaire was subjected to racist abuse on many occasions, even from very young children, no doubt taking their cue from their elders. As discussed earlier, the 1980s was a decade when racism was rife, and Black footballers, fewer in number than in modern-day football, were picked on by football fans, friend or foe. If things weren't going well for your own team, it was only too easy to pick on a Black player, and if the opposition had a Black player, he was guaranteed to be the target for abuse.

In Terry Venables, Palace had a manager who was younger than some players in the game, and he had plenty of new ideas and innovations to bring to the role. Ultimately, he had a wonderful career, which culminated in leading his national team. What if he had stayed at Palace for a bit longer? Instead, for some reason he departed for QPR, where he had great success with another 'unfashionable' club. Indeed, it was Venables who had built the young Palace team and turned them into prospective future champions, but the slide started with the sale of star player Peter Taylor to Spurs to balance the books at Selhurst Park. Despite that, it was under Venables that Palace reached the pinnacle of the First Division, but the bubble soon burst, and he went off to Loftus Road soon after.

Of course, he then went on to show what a great manager he was, taking unfancied QPR to the FA Cup Final, before becoming El Tel at Barcelona, winning La Liga and reaching the final of the Copa del Rey. A year later he led Barça to the European Cup Final, only to lose on penalties. Back in London, renewing his love affair with Tottenham Hotspur, Venables led them to FA Cup success in 1991 and finished third in the First Division in 1990, before taking over the England job four years later and coming so close to reaching the final of the Euros in 1996. Again, a case of what could have been at Palace if ...

Although Palace led the First Division in 1979/80, it was a very strong league, with the likes of Liverpool, Nottingham Forest, Aston Villa and Ipswich leading the way, so it was always going to be hard to compete at that level. And that's not even mentioning the likes of Everton and Manchester United, who were not at their peak just at that stage. However, Everton weren't far away from becoming top dogs in England, and they did that under Howard Kendall, another one that Palace let get away. Another 'what if' moment for the Palace faithful to ponder. However, it appears that Palace's keen interest in Kendall was the spark that saw Venables decide to leave his job. So they ended up with neither ... good work!

Even so, Palace were unbeaten in their first nine matches that season and all looked well until a dramatic decline in performance, which probably could be seen as starting with a 3-0 beating by Liverpool at Anfield to put the 'new boys' in their place. Perhaps the fact that this was such a young team meant that they couldn't deal with the pressure when results started to go against them. It's at times like this that there's no substitute for experience, and this young team had got so used to success. A poor end to the season saw Palace win just once in ten attempts, to finish 13th, and it was all downhill from there as you've read.

Chapter 14

What Happened Next?

THOSE OF you who don't know the history of Crystal Palace FC may wonder what all the fuss was about. After all, they're now a reasonably stable Premier League club, playing in the top flight of one of the strongest leagues in the world. They may not have won any major titles, and they're still very much a selling club but, unless your name is Leicester City, the likes of Palace, West Ham, Fulham, etc. usually start the season with modest ambitions. First it's about survival, then perhaps a top-half finish in a good season. Maybe even an early spot in the top six until the big boys take over (and Manchester City win the league!).

So rather than end on a negative note of 'what went wrong', let's briefly talk about what happened after the 80s. We left their story after a failed trip to Wembley, but perhaps things were on the up at the start of the 90s, as reaching the FA Cup Final for the first time and stabilising in their first season back in the big time was certainly encouraging. Steve Coppell had been in post for five years and was proving to be an astute young manager. Could this be the 'Team of the 90s?'

No doubt 1990/91 would have had people dreaming of that tag. Palace had their best-ever season, finishing an incredible third in the First Division, behind only Arsenal and Liverpool. This was no fluke either, as Palace were in the top four for the entire season and they had notable victories over Liverpool, Leeds and Spurs. Normally that would mean European football the following season, but Palace missed out due to the events of Heysel a few years before that led to a European ban on English clubs. Although the ban was now over, during that period English clubs' rankings had dropped, so there was only one UEFA Cup place up for grabs, and that, ironically, went to Liverpool for finishing as runners-up.

Although there was to be no repeat of Palace's feat in the FA Cup, and they also went out early in the League Cup, once again they were in the Full Members Cup, being run for the penultimate season. In the South region, after getting past Bristol Rovers of the Second Division, 2-1, Palace had a rare success at the Goldstone Ground, beating Brighton, also of the second tier, 2-0. This put the Eagles through to the semi-final and another glimpse of Wembley glory. First they had to get past top-tier Luton Town, but had a comfortable 3-1 victory at Selhurst Park, before meeting Norwich City in the South area final. The first leg at Carrow Road ended 1-1, so hopes were high that Palace, so strong at home this season, would finish the job and be back on their way to Wembley. On 10 March the Eagles booked their place in the final by defeating the Canaries 2-0 for their second Wembley final in as many years.

There was no impact on Palace's league form either, although they never quite got in touch with the top two to mount a title challenge. However, at this stage they were well clear of Leeds in fourth, with the likes of Manchester United, Manchester City, Wimbledon, Spurs and Everton all trailing behind. And it was Everton that Palace were to face on 7 April at Wembley in front of over 52,000 people in the final of the Full Members Cup.

Palace fans were said to outnumber those of Everton by two to one, and they saw a dour and physical affair, with the closest either team came to scoring in the first half being an Andy Gray free kick that hit Everton's crossbar. Palace took the lead on 66 minutes through a Geoff Thomas header, but just three minutes later the Toffees hit back through Robert Warzycha. No further goals came, so once again Palace faced extra time at Wembley.

This time, though, they finished the job ... and in some style. In the 101st minute Ian Wright put Palace ahead, followed 12 minutes later by a John Salako goal to make it 3-1. Just two minutes later Wright got his second to seal an emphatic 4-1 victory. Okay, it may not be a major cup competition, but it was still silverware and Palace had the satisfaction of climbing those famous Wembley steps to collect the cup.

Palace finished their season with an emphatic 3-0 victory over Manchester United at Selhurst Park, to show just how far they had come since moving into the top tier under Steve Coppell. Hopes must have been sky-high of more success to come in the years to follow.

The season of 1991/92 was to be a controversial one at Palace, brought about by a Channel 4 documentary, *Critical Eye – Great Britain United*, featuring interviews with some of the club's personnel. Given the problem with racism in the UK, not least within the football world, Palace's chairman, Ron Noades, stoked the fires by stating that Black footballers, although very skilful, needed White players alongside them to 'give the team some brains and common sense'. Unsurprisingly, Noades claimed that his words had been taken out of context, but the damage had been done, whichever way he meant it.[8]

Ian Wright left the club soon after, taking his goalscoring skills to Arsenal, where he would become a raging success and a cult hero. Without Wright, Palace went on to finish tenth in the First Division, a respectable position but, given the heights of the previous season, a disappointment. There was to be no silverware in the cup competitions either.

Crystal Palace FC became one of the founding 22 clubs of the new Premier League in 1992/93, and this time it was Ian Wright's strike partner, Mark Bright, who would be playing elsewhere, as he was

---

8 Duncan, John. 'Noades Still Under Fire', *The Guardian*, 17 September 1991.

sold to Sheffield Wednesday. Without their two key scorers of the previous few seasons, Palace struggled for goals, managing just 48 in their 42 league matches. As Manchester United won the first of their many Premier League titles, it was disaster for Palace, who finished 20th and were relegated to the First Division on goal difference, by just two goals. The only bright spot of the season was a good run in the League Cup that took the Eagles as far as the semi-finals. Unfortunately, there they met Arsenal, and old boy Ian Wright, who scored in both legs as the Gunners comfortably won 5-1 on aggregate and went on to lift the trophy against Mark Bright's Sheffield Wednesday.

After nine years at the club, after bringing back top-tier football, Steve Coppell saw relegation as his sign to go, and he was succeeded by his assistant, Alan Smith. The new man brought immediate success, showing that Palace deserved to be a Premier League club by storming to the First Division title in 1993/94, seven points clear of their nearest rivals, and scoring 73 league goals.

Back in the top flight for 1994/95, Palace found it tough in the league but had two great cup runs to the semi-finals. In the League Cup they eventually succumbed over two legs to eventual winners Liverpool, losing 1-0 at home and away. In the FA Cup it was Manchester United again, and another replay defeat. After drawing the first match at Villa Park 2-2, Palace went down 2-0 at the same venue in the replay. So close to two visits to Wembley in the same season. However, in the league, Palace were suffering from yo-yo syndrome, as they finished 19th and were relegated, once again struggling in front of goal, scoring just 34 times in 42 matches.

Once again, relegation was followed by the departure of the manager, as Smith left, to be replaced by Ray Lewington and Peter Nicholas as first-team coaches, with Steve Coppell returning in a technical director role at the club. Back in the second tier for 1995/96, it was to be heartbreak for Palace, who finished third in the league but were beaten in the play-off final at Wembley, 2-1 after extra time, by Leicester City. By this time Dave Bassett had been brought in as manager, but the following season, 1996/97, Palace slipped down to a sixth-placed finish, although this still meant a place in the play-offs. However, Bassett had already moved on before the end of the season, so Steve Coppell was back in charge. His team again reached the final at Wembley and this time made no mistake, beating Sheffield United by the only goal, scored by David Hopkin in the 90th minute. Coppell had taken his Palace team back to the Premier League for 1997/98.

It was to be a season that saw significant change at Selhurst Park. In February 1998, Mark Goldberg took over the club, having become a board member earlier in the season and been influential in bringing Attilio Lombardo and Michele Padovano to the club from Italy. However, they couldn't prevent Palace hitting rock bottom in the league by the time Goldberg took over, so Coppell moved upstairs to become Director of Football, while Lombardo took control of the team as player-manager. Unfortunately, this didn't lead to any improvement, and Palace finished bottom, relegated again. Lombardo had gone before the season ended.

Strangely, despite relegation and starting 1998/99 in the First Division, Palace entered the Intertoto Cup for their first taste of European football. A place in this competition wasn't earned by a high league finish, as those wishing to take part simply applied for a place, and Palace were England's highest-ranked club showing any interest. And who would take Palace on this European adventure? None other than Terry Venables, making his return to the club. However, it was a brief foray into the dream of European glory, as Palace lost 4-0 on aggregate in their first tie, against Samsunspor of Turkey.

More importantly, Goldberg lasted about as long as some recent Palace managers, as he couldn't financially back the club. Palace went into administration, Venables went and Steve Coppell took over once again. Palace was now a club in crisis, and there was to be no return to the riches of the Premier League, as they finished in mid-table in 1998/99 and had early cup exits. With Coppell in charge for 1999/00, Palace again finished mid-table.

Before 2000/01 kicked off, Jerry Lim purchased the club but then immediately sold it on to Simon Jordan, a millionaire Palace supporter. He replaced Coppell with a returning Alan Smith, in what was becoming a management merry-go-round. But in the league, things went from bad to worse for Palace and they very nearly ended up in the third tier, finishing just one point and one place above the relegation places. It took an 87th-minute goal on the last day of the season to save the Eagles from the drop. They did, though, have a good run in the League Cup, once again coming up against Liverpool in the semi-finals. In the first leg they once again got the better of the Reds, winning 2-1 at Selhurst Park, but at Anfield it was a completely different story, Liverpool thrashing Palace 5-0 for a comfortable aggregate victory.

Given Palace's poor league form, Smith had already been shown the door before the season ended, replaced by Steve Kember on a temporary basis for the final two matches, both of which they won, which meant First Division football for 2001/02. But it was not to be Kember in charge, as Steve Bruce was given the role. He didn't last long either, as he left for Birmingham City, with Trevor Francis coming the other way to take charge at Selhurst Park. Despite the management uncertainties, it was a better season, ending in a tenth-place finish, so Palace actually had the same manager at the start of the next season.

It was another mid-table finish in 2002/03, however, and Francis left once the season was over. Finally, Steve Kember was given the main job, but he was not to see out 2003/04, sacked in November after a poor run of form that left Palace looking at the drop to the third tier. In December, former Palace player Iain Dowie took over and transformed their season. Remarkably, Palace finished sixth, bagging the final play-off spot. Not only that but they reached the final at Cardiff's Millennium Stadium, being used for domestic cup finals during the Wembley rebuild. A goal by captain Neil Shipperley was enough to see off West Ham and book Palace a place back in the Premier League.

Unfortunately, it was a difficult return in 2004/05, and Palace finished 18th, so again dropped to the second tier, now called the Championship. It was their fourth relegation from the Premier League. However, faith was shown in Dowie, who remained in charge for 2005/06, and he led his team to sixth place and the play-offs again. Unfortunately they went down to Watford in the semi-finals, so faced another season in the second tier. They also lost manager Dowie, replaced by former fan favourite Peter Taylor for 2006/07.

There was to be no glorious return for Taylor, as Palace slipped back to mid-table. Although he still led Palace at the start of 2007/08, after only two months it was his turn to leave, with Neil Warnock replacing him in the hot seat. He led Palace to fifth place by the end of the season but it was another play-off semi-final defeat, this time to Bristol City. Having improved Palace's form, hopes would have been high for 2008/09, but they dropped down to 15th in a disappointing season.

Financial woes returned in 2009/10, as a transfer embargo was placed on the club at the start of the season, due to monies owed to other clubs for transfer fees. In January 2010 Palace entered administration again and started to sell off some key players to make ends meet. Neil Warnock also left to take over at QPR, so Paul Hart was appointed as a caretaker manager for the rest of the season. On the pitch, things were going well early in the season, but Palace also faced a ten-point deduction for their financial performance, so were again facing the drop to the third tier. And again it was final-day heroics that saved them, as they salvaged a 2-2 draw with Sheffield Wednesday that saw their opponents relegated instead.

Before 2010/11 commenced, a consortium of Palace fans secured the freehold of Selhurst Park, and they also appointed a new manager, George Burley, who had previously led his native Scotland. With a depleted squad it was always going to be difficult for the new man, who only lasted 25 matches into the season before being replaced by his assistant Dougie Freedman. In what was a struggle of a season, at least Palace fans were saved the stress of a last-match drama, as their team secured Championship status with one match to spare.

With Freedman in charge for 2011/12, Palace's final league position improved to 17th; not startling, but at least not facing the threat of relegation. And once again they had a good run in the League Cup, reaching the semi-finals, having knocked out Manchester United in the quarter-finals. With a place in the final at Wembley against Liverpool or Manchester City beckoning, Palace faced fellow Championship club Cardiff City in the semi-final. The first leg at Selhurst Park raised Palace fans' hopes as they won 1-0, with a goal by Anthony Gardner. He then scored again in the second leg, but this time an own goal, as Cardiff won 1-0 to take the tie to extra time. After no further goals, it was a penalty shoot-out, but Palace failed miserably from the spot to lose 3-1.

Unusually in recent times, Palace had the same man in charge for the third season in a row, although Freedman was not there for much longer, moving on to Bolton Wanderers a couple of months into the campaign. Next up in the permanent role was Ian Holloway, who won his first match 5-0, which saw Palace sitting top of the table. Unfortunately, it didn't last, but Palace finished fifth and entered the play-offs once more. After disposing of Brighton in the semi-finals, it was off to Wembley to face favourites Watford. The final ended 0-0 and went into extra time, where a Kevin Phillips penalty was enough to see Palace back in the big time … if only they could stay there this time.

After a poor start to 2013/14, Holloway quit, to be replaced by Tony Pulis, who led Palace to a respectable 11th, well clear of any relegation worries. Could Palace now establish themselves as a Premier League club? Certainly not under Pulis, who left just before 2014/15 kicked off, with Neil Warnock returning for a second spell in charge. However, he had gone before 2015 rang in. In January, former player, and FA Cup semi-final hero, Alan Pardew became Palace's manager and their form improved, finishing tenth by the season's end.

Palace were now playing their third consecutive season in the top tier and looked to have established themselves at last. Although finishing a lowly 15th in the table, 2015/16 will be remembered for Palace reaching their second FA Cup Final. Having been fortunate in the draw in their previous foray to the final, this time Palace were made to work harder, beating Premier League clubs Southampton, Stoke and Spurs in their first three ties. In the quarter-final they defeated Championship club Reading away for a place in the semi-final at Wembley against top-tier Watford. Goals by Yannick Bolasie and Connor Wickham were enough to give Palace a 2-1 victory and a place in the final, where they had the opportunity for revenge against Manchester United, who had spoiled their dream 26 years previously.

On 26 May 2016 United did it again, winning 2-1 after extra time, but not before Palace had given them a mighty scare. It looked like ending goalless over 90 minutes, but Jason Puncheon gave the Eagles the lead on 78 minutes. Just 12 minutes to hang on, but typically United hit back, Juan Mata scoring with a deflected shot just three minutes later. Despite United being reduced to ten men in extra time when Chris Smalling was sent off, Jesse Lingard hit their winner with five minutes remaining. Again for Palace it was a case of missed opportunity for glory.

The following season was spent in the lower half of the Premier League, which led to the dismissal of Alan Pardew in December, replaced by Sam Allardyce. Palace finished 14th, but Big Sam left at the end of the season. Palace then appointed their first foreign manager, former Netherlands international Frank de Boer, to start 2017/18. Perhaps it was the attempt to implement a different style of football from that of Allardyce, with the same squad of players, but De Boer's appointment soon turned into a disaster, and he wasn't given time to rectify it. An opening-day defeat at home to Huddersfield by 3-0 was perhaps an ominous sign. This was followed by three further losses: away at Liverpool, at home to Swansea and away at Burnley. No points from four matches, and De Boer was sacked.

In came Roy Hodgson, 70 years old, but with bags of experience. Three further defeats followed in the league – Southampton, Manchester City and Manchester United, with nine goals shipped in the latter two. But more patience was shown with Hodgson, despite Palace sitting bottom of the table after setting a record of seven defeats in their first seven matches and not yet finding the net. Palace fans must have feared the worst, but under Hodgson things soon picked up and the Eagles finished a very respectable 11th by the end of the season. He then established his Palace team as a steady mid-table performer over the next three seasons, with finishes of 12th, 14th and 14th but he then left at the end of his contract.

Before the start of 2021/22, Palace appointed Frenchman Patrick Vieira, who had a good first season at Selhurst Park. Again it was a mid-table finish, but Palace had their first good cup run for a few years, reaching the semi-finals of the FA Cup, but then losing out to Chelsea. Early promise again led to disappointment, though, as Vieira's second season didn't last the full term. After a run of 12 matches without a win he was gone, with Palace battling relegation for the first time in several seasons. The call went out to Roy Hodgson to perform his miracles to save Palace's season once more. He didn't disappoint, taking them up to 11th place and yet another mid-table finish in 2022/23.

All of which brings up to the current season as I write. Hodgson was only supposed to step in for the rest of the previous season to steady the sinking ship, but 2023/24 saw him appointed in a permanent role. However, due to ill health, he was forced to step down in February 2024. His replacement was Oliver Glasner, and the Austrian has been doing a fine job, with Palace firmly established as a mid-table Premier League club, having beaten Liverpool (at Anfield!), West Ham (5-2!) and Newcastle United in April 2024. They have a promising young team, with some special flair players, such as Mark Guéhi, Michael Olise and Eberechi Eze. Unfortunately, the big clubs are already casting a keen eye on some of these players, but if Palace can hang on to them, who knows; perhaps there are better times ahead ...

Acknowledgements

THERE ARE so many people to thank when writing a book. Above all I want to thank my father, Richard Brandt, who helped nurture my love for the sport, and is always willing to listen to me drone on about some random fact on Palace that seems earth-shattering to me at the time. Unfortunately, he died before this book went to press. England in the late 70s to early 80s has always been an era in my family that we reminisce about. Following two books on South America, I felt in my bones that a book based on an English club was overdue.

Thanks to my good friends Mateo and Amanda Escobar, who have always been fans. Also to Duffy Alverson, who has been my co-host on the 'Subs Bench' for almost five years.

Crystal Palace answered many questions quickly whenever I could pepper them with something I was stuck on. Chris Lee from 'Outsidewrite' always has something in his books, podcast or blog that can be used in anything. The editors of *The Football Pink*, *Football Paradise* and *These Football Times* have the most in-depth writing I can find anywhere. Thanks also to Andy Caulton, a Brit expat living in New Hampshire, who knows the sport better than most, and John Spurling for his great book that I referred to a lot. My editing has always started with Aaron Rozek, and extra information was provided by Morgan Michie. Jim Piddock was a great help for some extra information.

Finally, thanks to all at Pitch Publishing for helping me get this book out there!

The Author

STEPHEN BRANDT has written all over the world on nostalgia, the game of football and opinion recaps. He has hosted football podcasts going back to 2011, and had guest spots on other podcasts worldwide. He currently lives in the north-east of the United States. He has a Bachelor of Arts Degree in Modern European Military History from the University of Kansas and a Masters in Sports Administration from Canisius. This is his second book with Pitch Publishing, following 2023's *Flamengo: Winning All the Cups*.

Bibliography

Burridge, John. *Budgie: The Autobiography of Goalkeeping Legend.* (London: John Blake Publishing, 2013)

Butler, Ivan. *Liverpool Matches of My Life: From Second Division to World Champions.* (Worthing: Pitch Publishing, 2020)

Crooks, Richard. *What Was Football Like in the 1980s?* (Worthing: Pitch Publishing, 2020)

Gilroy, Paul. *There Ain't No Black in the Union Jack: The Cultural Politics of Race and Nation.* (Chicago: University of Chicago Press, 1987)

Goldblatt, David. *The Ball is Round: A Global History of Soccer.* (New York, Penguin, 2006)

Higgins, Simon. *Dark Days to Cup Finals: A Supporter's Story of Crystal Palace FC 1981–1993.* (Simon Higgins Self Publish: New Haven Connecticut, 2021)

Hilaire, Vince. *The Autobiography of Vince Hilaire.* (London: Biteback Publishing, 2018)

Lee, Chris. *Origin Stories. The Pioneers Who Took Football to the World.* (Worthing: Pitch Publishing, 2021)

Purkins, Mike. *Crystal Palace: A Complete Record 1905–1989.* (Derby: Breedon Books Sports, 1989)

Sands, Rev. Nigel. *Crystal Palace Football Club: One Hundred of the Finest Matches.* (Cheltenham: Tempus Publishing Ltd, 2002)

Spurling, Jon. *Get it On: How the '70s Rocked Football.* (London: Biteback Publishing, 2021)

Tossell, David. *All Crazee Now: English Football and Footballers in the 1970s.* (Worthing: Pitch Publishing, 2021)

Tossell, David. *Big Mal: The High Life and Hard Times of Malcolm Allison, Football Legend.* (Edinburgh: Mainstream Publishing, 2008)

Venables, Terry. *Venables: The Autobiography.* (London: Penguin Publishing, 1995)

Wilson, Jonathan. *Inverting the Pyramid: History of Soccer Tactics* (New York City: Bold Type Books, 2018)

Websites, Magazines, Programmes, TV Shows

BT Sport Films – *Team of the Eighties*

Crystal Palace FC: *The Last Ten Years. There And Back Again* – club programme

Daily Mail

The Guardian

Over the Bar

The Eagles Beak

Five Year Plan

Holmesdale Online

Late Tackle

Crystal Palace website

when saturday comes magazine

Game of the People
Football Paradise
The Football Pink
These Football Times
Brighton and Hove Independent
The Set Pieces
The National Archives
Past Tense Blog
Tale of Two Halves
The Goldstone Wrap
Football.London